PERFORMANCE BANKING AND RURAL DEVELOPMENT

PERFORMANCE BANKING AND RURAL DEVELOPMENT

Somu Giriappa

2004

DAYA PUBLISHING HOUSE

Delhi - 110 035

ISBN 81-7035-325-4

Published by : **Daya Publishing House**
1123/74, Deva Ram Park
Tri Nagar, Delhi - 110 035
Phone : 27383999
Fax : (011) 27382329
e-mail : dayabooks@vsnl.com
website : www.dayabooks.com

Showroom : 4762-63/23, Ansari Road, Darya Ganj,
New Delhi - 110 002
Phone: 23245578, 23244987

Laser Typesetting : **Classic Computer Services**
Delhi - 110 035

Printed at : **Chawla Offset Printers**
Delhi - 110 052

PRINTED IN INDIA

PREFACE

The Chair in Rural Banking and Management at the Mangalore University, jointly sponsored by SyndicateBank and Canara Bank, in its 8 years of existence has brought out a number of project reports and publications on diverse subjects like evaluation of rural development programmes, hitech agriculture including aquaculture, floriculture and animal husbandry, priority sector banking, small scale industries, agricultural marketing, impact of information technology on banks, evaluation of weaker section programmes, evaluation of IRDP and PMRY, SC/ST enterprises and housing programmes besides bringing out seminar proceedings on impact of science and technology on economic reforms and copyright law.

The Chair believes that the studies undertaken by it do find some relevance in the policy changes of the sponsoring banks and also to the economy.

In the completion of the reports, the unstinted support extended by the Mangalore University, SyndicateBank and Canara Bank and their numerous branches and other governmental and non-governmental institutions in the region require special mention of appreciation. My colleagues in the department of Economics of the University deserve due acknowledgement for their wholehearted support and indulgence. To ever-available instant assistance provided by the Chair staff, Sri Ramesh Salian, Sri Seetharam, M and Ms Sushma K R, my thanks are due. The Mangalore Lead Bank Manager (SyndicateBank) Sri Anant Ram and his staff are to be thanked for providing computer data relating to banking progress in the Dakshina Kannada district which enabled us complete this study.

Finally, I wish to thank Sri Anil Mittal, proprietor of Daya Publishing House, who has come to my rescue many a time and for bringing out this publication like many others.

SOMU GIRIAPPA

EXECUTIVE SUMMARY

There have been some major changes in the structure of banking industry in the recent past owing to the globalization trends and communication and information technology. Indian banking also has been affected and various financial reform agendas have propped up the organization and performance of the different groups of banking. Banking performance can be evaluated by analyzing indicators like capital adequacy, asset quality, management quality, earnings quality, liquidity, non performance assets ratio and profit ratio, besides interest spread.

There have been many elements of risks, which have been encountered by the banks in the realm of market and prices besides value at risk and country, transfer and governance risks. When the proportion of non-performing assets is declining and interest spread is declining, that indicate a better performance of the banks and declining risks standards as defined by new Basel Accord. In many banks the risk weighted capital ratio has been showing an increase. While the performance of public sector banks has shown an improvement over the years because of the prudential norms adopted, the old private banks have had some problems while the new private banks have emerging problems. The public sector banks dominate the banking scenario, led by the State Bank group while the ICICI Bank leads the private sector banks, and Citibank leads the foreign banks. The share of foreign banks is still around 5 percent in total assets and other variables and these banks have been put into strains of late which has made some of the branches to near close-down.

Major banks in the Dakshina Kannada district are SyndicateBank, Canara Bank, Vijaya Bank, Corporation Bank, Karnataka Bank Ltd, SCDCC Bank, PCARD Bank, Netravati Grameen Bank and others. Priority sector advances accounted for over 80 percent in some taluks while in others it was upto 60 percent. Crop cultivation and SSI have been the important priority sectors, while the share of IRDP and PMRY has been very small in all the regions. When compared to 2000-01, the performance in 2001-02 has been slightly better off for the priority sectors, though there has been some slight variation in the performance of the major bank branches. Mangalore taluk accounts for the bulk of the demand and advances outstanding.

Given the type of intensive banking activation in the region, further inroads of the PSBs seems to be rather saturated while many private sector banks have been established with universal banking characteristics. A major problem in credit facilitation has been the declining credit-deposit ratio with higher level of investment which makes the commercial banks rather limited in their scope of furthering the cause of rural development. Hence a new strategy has to be worked out wherein the commercial banks and the cooperative and regional banks together will operate in an agglomerate way with an optimal area selection and also an optimal activity selection toward greater specialization and integration of both the spatial and functional linkages.

CONTENTS

1
INTRODUCTION TO RURAL DEVELOPMENT

Introduction

In any development process, base infrastructure is essential for any adoption of technology or restructure of the system. Transportation, power, raw materials, marketing and communication on the one hand and social infrastructure on the other become necessary initiatives for the planned growth of various sectors and groups. Whatever may be the superstructure, without an appropriate infrastructure, it will not yield the optimal results. Rural roads, including link roads have been important spatially integrating factors. The absence of full-fledged road system constraints other infrastructure adjuncts. The development of rural road system has been one of apathy and callousness oriented when the state of urban roads itself is ineffectual. These are huge investment requiring ventures requiring a long duration and systematic development. The attention given by the present employment programmes to link infrastructure development and self-employment activities is far from sustainable when the quantity and quality of the works are considered. It is a case where everything is included for development but none is developed, owing to not only unsustainable investment but also due to untimely and ineffective utilisation of the resources. The problem becomes one of properly matching labour and technology inputs, which becomes difficult owing to administered and less than sustainable factor prices.

Though there has been a growth of modern transportation system, the traditional system is still predominant; the problem does not arise from this perspective. The neglect of the traditional system intensifies the problem. Same is the case with regard to rural industrialization and communication, which have been subject to long time discrimination. Wherever measures have been undertaken, they have been in the sphere of administrative or political decisions. So long as the rural sector was less marketed, the need for long distance transportation was not felt necessary in the rural areas, but the growth of magnetization process has proved crucial in strengthening the linkage effect. Rural transportation is still the problem of the private sector, in that the rural inhabitants themselves have to plan their transportation process due to lack of adequate public support system in the matter.

Irrigation, storage and organized marketing, input support systems, credit and other inputs unless made available in adequate quantity and quality in the right time and to the right people, become less effectual and subject to vicissitudes of profiteering participation. The several programmes which aim at directed credit to the target groups forget about the importance of infrastructure; if they do, the superstructure would be tried to be built in the absence of proper infrastructure. This brings to the fore the nature of prioritization which should be followed in programming the change. The basic economic infrastructure deficiency bothering the rural areas has been lack of income generating asset creation directly or indirectly and those, which could improve the skill formation of the rural people. Among the social infrastructures again skill improvement health and sanitation facilities are lacking, besides educational appropriation. People's participation, the crucial political-oriented infrastructure is yet to emerge in an efficient alternative to the existing dependency syndrome. As regards institutional infrastructure, the existing institutions have become subsidiaries of government departments or have turned defunct owing to their narrow perspective and short-term profiteering policies. Development administration, as fallout of the colonial model increases only officialdom resulting in dependency and alienation of the masses from the decision making process. The various planning strategies adopted have resulted in weak institutional framework for development of the disadvantaged groups.

The Efficacy of the Programmes

A programme is not a charity work undertaken by the bureaucrats or the urbanites to the rural people. It is a planned activity supplementing the sector development process and thus aims at transforming the different sectors and regions. The programmes are dynamic enough to infuse the desired level of change in the traditional system so as to enable it realize a reasonable level of growth like the modern sector. It has become customary to blame infrastructure facilities, the weakness of other programmes and the apathy of the rural population for failure of the development programmes in the rural areas. It is like the defeated political party blaming the opposition's machination and the people's changing preferences. For any failure, the programme itself has to be blamed. If its organization and structure were to be efficient, its functions can be made more effective resulting in a better performance. Properly planning and formulating the structure, functions and performance of any programme leads to its wholesome and integrated process of justification and incorporation into the existing tools. A programme is a solution to a problem and unless the problem is systematically studied and evaluated, the programme in question may not be able to address fully to the needs of the situation. Basic needs are having the base infrastructure for development, but performance is the crucial element in the process. Programmes, which are conceived of political decisions, cannot be stabilized by economic factors unless there are common and positive linkage effects between the two. A programme is the link between the planning process and the delivery system and hence shall be a well-structured one appropriate to the given situation or an aggregation of the same. Not only the quantum of assistance under the programme which matters for its effectiveness, but quality aspects count equally important. They include their suitability, stability, productivity, optimality, sustainability, equity and integrity. Of course, fulfillment of all these requisites simultaneously may be difficult and like the general growth process, it is a step by step development process and unless this perspective is kept intact, the resulting integration will be weak and biased.

Revival of the rural growth process has to depend on parameters like adequate capital formation for all the subgroups, risk coverage, minimized wastage and damage, better return on assets, adequate returns for further investment and a sustained growth of the rural activity. From this perspective, various land and human development restructuring activities have concentrated on mergers, better privatization and corporate initiatives and people's planning. This requires decontrol of the sector from various exigencies and encouragement of local area development through a consortium of institutions, of course, hinged upon viable propositions. The curative actions have to concentrate on cleansing the existing institutions and making them more responsible and development-oriented, whereas the preventive measures would demand such measures so as to enable disintermediation for self-organization and securitization for asset improvement. A rational construct requires the assumption of complete rationality among the masses and effecting choices in accordance with set goals and privileges.

Institutions working in the field of rural development may be development oriented or motivated through political or religious compulsions toward social change. In such cases, they may behave as political or religious parties and their organization and performance will be aptly tuned to reach such of those goals only. Here, both governmental and non-governmental institutions may have similar objectives irrespective of their organizational and performance structures. Since it is the NGOs who specialize in the latter process, their technology adoption process may exhibit elements of both as the planners or implementers as the case may or as participants realizing their own objectives. The proportion of development NGOs may be very small, if the returns from participation and articulation may not be adequate to justify their existence. That does not mean that they exist only to flourish themselves; it would economically unjustifiable if the elements, which are incorporated in any programmes, are not the focus of the NGOs also. The purpose of the voluntary institutions in providing an effective alternative to the existing weak organization of the programmes by government with service orientation is slowly changing into one of commercial venture, just like politics or religion.

In the age of globalization where deepening of institutional structure requires integration and interdependency with many others, the organizational framework of the institutions has to dwell on globally competitive-oriented market strategy. Increasing the possibility for externalization and redistribution of participate benefits have to be incorporated into the institutional property rights so that the property markets become interrelated and the institutions become professional. Since long the appropriateness of institutions in rural development ahs been much debated and hence choice of institutions has to centre on the local specifics and the price of institution building process. There could be diversity and pluralism in the institutional development process and this has to consider the type of technology that could be developed in the areas of social, political and economic fields, such as empowerment, economic development, service and special coverage prospects.

Rural Development and Technological Change

Technology has been looked down as an evil, subversive and as a debilitating force not only in the developing but also in the developed countries. The reason for the latter has been the overemphasis given to it till the quality aspects of technology began to be questioned from the early seventies. In the developing countries, the problem ensues due to the import dilemma- what not to import, how not to use and the like. When technology, conceived and generated with reference to the social, economic and geographical conditions of the developed countries, seldom becomes matching in the developing countries. The fact that the tropics bear the brunt of underdevelopment is amply proved by the ever continuous reproduction of all living organisms due to lack of winter termination of predators, pests, diseases and weeds of crops and the resulting growth of 'bads' over years. The over-dependence on rainfall for major landuse and crop use patterns further deteriorates the soil structure and the need to larger amendments, which may not be forthcoming due to infrastructure and investment problems. When the technologies are transferred to the developing systems without properly understanding the conditions there (which has been the practice), no wonder the impact becomes sub-optimal and ineffective. This applies not only to import of physical technology in various fields like agriculture, animal husbandry, health and industries but also in the case of social technology in the areas of community development, communication and participation. The imported technology has been largely centralized and problem resolving rather than decentralized and problem solving appropriate to the specific situations. The intensity of governance also fortified the centric approach such that innovative participation lost its appeal.

Between the existing technology and the imported technology packages- in the fields of biological, mechanical, chemical, information and management innovations, consistency problems arose. Some were redundant in that similar results emerged and in some there were conflicts among the two when the results happened to be contradictory. Though the advantages of the new technology were proved definitely superior to the locals, their social acceptability norms were diluted and sometimes ignored. This resulted in slow adoption of the technologies at the same time, the process of adaptation and innovation remaining almost non-existent. Since absorptive capacity depends on individual capacity for technology adaptation and institutional framework for technological development, application of the general principles of technical progress in creating a cadre of problem solving technologies and innovators become crucial. Otherwise, impact of technology in poverty alleviation will be ineffective, as has been the case so far.

In order to make technology more effective in delivering poverty amelioration; adoption of social transformation technologies and creation of community leadership in problem solving and suitably tailoring the technology to suit local conditions has to be the focus of the technology programmes. Transfer of local technologies is impossible, since none such thing exists. They have to be created indigenously with problem solving skills. The transfer process and the programmes have to address themselves to this task more so rather than resolving the crisis now and then depending on the intensity and pressure tactics of the interest groups. Once the problem solving skill becomes embodied into the population, the influence of the interest groups will be subject to checks and balances. Technology has the capacity to reduce poverty both directly and indirectly and this process depends on the nature of technological change, the structure of poverty, the structure of the rural economy and the socio-political framework in which it is enveloped. The green revolution technology has had significant effects and its second coming may further intensify the process of transformation. The nexus between technology and rural development then focuses on amiable intervention to maximize poverty reduction, assessable for every individual case. Direct effects may reduce aggregate poverty in an agrarian economy like ours. But when there are a large number of small and marginal households this becomes a problematic issue in covering such a huge proportion of rural population and hence indirect effects are also have relevance. The general growth process is the indirect effect whereas direct poverty alleviation programmes may supplement that. Further, targeting technological changes across different crops and rural activities will improve the productivity levels in the rural sector. This over a period of time will reduce agricultural prices, which then will be in a position to reduce urban poverty levels also.

Technological effects when they are mooted indirectly to benefit the poor farmers by the principle of non-exclusion will have the facilitation of social aggregation thereby mitigating their status problems. in this, employment generation effect of technology assumes importance both in a direct and indirect way. However, the distribution of gains from direct and indirect effects of technology depends on the specific rural cluster; here integration from the viewpoint of functions and activities will pave the way for social cohesion and creation of what is called a 'social bloc' to facilitate accumulation of social capital and through this generation of social technology. Improvement of production system, employment generation and increase in agricultural productivity are to be the main focus of any rural development programmes aimed through technological change. If the agricultural income could be increased and at the same time with a declining food prices (the targeted public distribution system notwithstanding where bulk of the food subsidy is eaten away in storage of huge buffer stocks), it may diversify the activities to such an extent that there will be a diversified food consumption pattern not only among the urban poor but also among the rural poor. Only when the ratio of agricultural exports increase that the appreciation of rupee may take place leading to augmentation of this price effect to all the commodities. Though agriculture is a declining industry, only in its rejuvenation that the future of growth of the economy depends.

Rural development thus became interdisciplinary infused with many a concept. Nonetheless, technology was looked upon as saviour of humanity in a competitive world and its impact has been caricatured in terms of non-human effects on the developed countries and as inhuman effects on the developing countries by different parodies. Ever since Solow and Abromowitz established the residual, technology and total factor productivity have assumed the status of engine of development in all the countries. Of course, before accentuating on the tentacles of technology, resource mobilization has to be given its due place, for growth is linear and systematic rather than a haphazard and quick burning fuel. Where contribution of technology is difficult to be measured owing to already embodied capital or disembodied labour, the residual becomes incognito; in such circumstances, capital accumulation gets a lead which in the long run may be subject to entropical effects. The pitfalls of the recently developed countries experiencing economic crises amply proves the fallacy of accumulation as contrasted to efficiency augmentation and in this, both have their due role to play in sustaining an economy in the long run (Krugman 1994).

When the applicability of world growth models was questioned for the developing countries' referencing, the appropriate technology movement based on the Gandhian self-reliance ideology was proclaimed to be more humane in approach for the poor countries beset with structural problems. As such, rural development was considered as an alternate model of development especially meant for the developing nations. Appropriate choice and adaptation of technology with the given absorptive capacity would generate more equitable and less elusive development; it was argued (Wolfe 1996). Meanwhile, environment became more important than economic development and the green shift in paradigm was complete. The rich countries, owing to their already developed nature, could devote efforts toward environmental sustainment, whereas the poor countries, before achieving a reasonable level of development, have been called upon to toe the lines of the world order; hence the conflict between the two aspects of development jeopardizes the stability of the poor countries in many spheres. This type of dependency models- in the sense of poor countries depending on the rich through spillover or trickle-down effect and also the primary sectors depending on the secondary and tertiary sectors for sustained development- gave rise to the institutionalization of appropriate technology, taking a middle path of growth strategy. In this, exploitation of weak sectors and economies by the strong ones was not without blemishes, though it was argued in the long run, the effects will balance each other toward achieving a smooth process of renovating technology on the one hand by the rich countries and import of frontier technology on the other by the poor countries. Of course, this experiment was at a huge cost and has created a widening gap between the two over the years. The share of the top 20 percent of the rich in world income has increased from 69.5 percent in 1960 to 83.4 percent in 1990 (Korzeniewicz and Moran 1997), indicating a declined share of the poor. The other reason given for this widening gap is the growing difference between the new (cheese and butter, characterized by technology stocks) and the old (the brick and mortar) economy. Regarding poverty alleviation in poor countries, those who advocate a technocratic approach emphasize the role of targets and reallocation of resources with proper policy design as distinguished from the institutionalizes who argue about the leading role played by various social institutions in the programme success (Besley 1997). However, targeting may be more efficient in advanced countries, whereas the institutional approach may be relevant to poor countries.

When growth became fumbled and technology prejudiced, how the institutions have acted, as carriers of development in the poor countries- is a mute question vigorously debated by (under-?) development economists. Institutional approach normally takes either the centralization or decentralization route depending upon the structure of the economy and its performance. If development through macro initiatives would be time-consuming, an effective decentralized strategy could induct both social justice and self-reliance as has been experienced by countries like China. However, with growing intensity of overgovernance by the centralized sector and apathetic performance of the decentralized sector, development becomes less recursive and the institutions in the process are turned ineffective and partial. A vigorous technology and institution building mechanism to effect transformation of the factor and product markets reinforced by economic reforms becomes an essential ingredient of policy.

2
BANKING INDUSTRY

Introduction

The banking industry in India is facing unprecedented competition from non-traditional banking institutions, which now offer banking and financial services over the internet. The deregulation of the banking industry coupled with the emergence of new technologies, are enabling new competitors to enter the financial services market quickly and efficiently. Indian banks are going for the retail banking in a big way. However, much is still to be achieved. According to a study of Indian Institute of Management, Lucknow, throughout the country, the Internet Banking is in the nascent stage of development (only 50 banks are offering varied kind of internet banking services) in general, these internet sites offer only the most basic services. Features on infotech use include internet banking, e-banking, banking on IT, internet syndications, director services, information technology bill and its implications and issues, minimum acceptable tolerance for software (MATS), banking computerization, branch networking: are banks on the right track and survey on the performance of Indian software and service exports, besides technological developments in banking.

It was in fifties that the government of India evolved the policy of using the banking system as an instrument of economic development and social change and, as a first step, the SBI was given the mandate of a massive branch expansion programme and was asked to open branches in far-flung unbanked areas and assist in their development. This resulted in an explosion of sorts in volumes of transactions and posed a severe strain on all resources. More particularly, the inter-branch reconciliation became one area that defied manual handling. It was in this background that the first steps towards mechanization was taken by installing what was known as ICL 40 column punched card equipment in late fifties and early sixties in the Kolkata office of the SBI for the reconciliation of inter branch transactions.

The pace of branch expansion was so fast that by early sixties this equipment was also considered inadequate and the bank went in for the first computer-an IBM 1401 supported by a battery of about one hundred 80-column punched card machines for data input. The whole system of reporting and reconciliation of transactions was revamped and modernized. Other larger nationalized Banks also followed suit. Interestingly, at that time, no immediate need was felt for automation of branch and customer related activities or for that matter head office / corporate office operations. The banking system went in for massive employment drives. Most of the banking being of mandated kind, quality inputs in the form of analyzed data were neither envisaged nor considered necessary. MIS was still in its infancy, RBI and SBI made some efforts to develop MIS in the area of deposit and advances through use of Uniform Balance Books etc. which finally matured in the form of Basic Statistical Returns. By the seventies, committee reports had started talking in terms of industrial databases.

Another significant development that had a bearing on the bank computerization was the advent of personal computers in the eighties and their easy availability. As time passed on, volumes increased further and manual handling of these volumes led to dwindling customer service and increasing complaints. With increased trade unionism and rather restrained handling of available human resources, a realization grew that unless computerization of customer accounts and other banking services like remittances etc. at branch level was resorted to, things will go out of hand. However, mechanization of any kind was opposed by the unions and resulted in slowing down of computerization drive in Indian banks.

Front office mechanization where front desk operations were computerized while back office work was done manually and back office automation covering mechanization of general ledger and back office operations while the front office work was done manually.

Both the models provided the customer with error-free accounting, regular statements of accounts etc. Considering the contemporary level of computerization, these were major achievements but did not go far enough and the pace of their implementation was tardy, to say the least, with not a little opposition from trade unions.

Many countries have been afflicted with the Dutch disease wherein a boom in the resource sector results in resource movements among different sectors leading to expansion of the service sector (deindustrialization). Also, there is the risk of resource curse especially when a particular resource is put into overuse in which case it loses its productivity growth and becomes a burden to development in the long run. Therefore, the long-term effects of such a structural change resulting from addition of resources are far from conclusive. Many countries which had seen increase in mineral resources have experienced this disease. The contribution of the service sector to GDP in more developed countries has been above the world average of 65 per cent. Even the primary and secondary sector has a significant tertiary component in them.

The emerging pattern of globalization induced by communication and information technology and international relations declared by world bodies such as would trade organization and others have further intensified the tertiary economy. A more toward few trade and compliance to the general agreement on trade and services will enthuse greater private participation thus weaning away state control in all the commercial sectors. Banking has been one of the leading sectors to be globally networked owing to its size and spread and be treated as an industry.

The recent trend of giant banking corporations and holding companies has made them leading asset holders in the world. The multinational banks have acquired a globalized culture. At the same time universal banking where different activities like banking, insurance and securities are continued under one umbrella has also been spreading its wings. So much so the present day bank bas to be competitive not only with other banks but also with insider houses. There have been many bank failures and mergers and acquisitions, which have resulted in shrinkage of members and consolidation.

The history of banking progress has not been a smooth one and the sector had to face many restrictions inspite of the protected calls. Three years and with a new trend by liberalized growth, the economy has to face many challenges. In the process standardization becomes difficult to be enforced upon. According to the Basel Accord of 2001 the rigidities in capital requirements have been liberalized and the scope for capital arbitrage and increased sophistication in the measurement and management of risk has been extended. The new accord brings upon minimum capital requirements, processes of supervisory review and market display (Jalan 2002). Improving the measurement of risks of market and credit has been focused to set targets for capital adequacy. The implementation of the accord would require increased capital and development of efficient internal system for assessment and management of risks and improving internal contents. This will result in enhancement of technical skills to handle new technologies and risks.

Risks in Banking

Bank risk has been termed the major focus in global banking and has resulted in their detailed analysis, assessment and management. According to the Narasimham Committee on Banking Sector Reforms (1998) capital adequacy requirement should consider market risks in addition to credit risks. Credit risk is the probability that a borrower will fail to meet banks' obligations to meet commitments with reference to lending, trading, hedging, settlement and other financial transactions. It is made up of transaction or default risk and portfolio risk. The portfolio risk comprising intransigent and concentration risk depends on both external (state of the economy, fluctuation in prices, exchange rates) interest rates etc) and internal portions (loan policy, appraisal of borrowers financial position, adequacy in risk pricing, loan review mechanism, lending limits and others). The banks have to assess, and manage the default risks as part of the credit delivery process. The risk involves inability or unwillingness of the borrower to meet the commitments. The internal risk, inherent in particular line of business may be relatively low (scale as housing finance) or high (as in software finance). The concentration risk is defined in terms of borrowers) geography, lines of business and industries. For this quantitative ceiling of aggregate exposure in specified categories of borrowers and evaluation of the ratingwise distribution becomes essential.

Because of globalization and openness of the economy the banks have to face new risks in order to compete globally. In respect of risk rating, the Reserve Bank of India directs that the banks should have a comprehensive risk rating system that serves as a single point indication of diverse risk factors of a counter party and for taking decision in a consistent manner. The risk rating system has to be devised so as to reveal the overall risk of lending which becomes the critical input for price setting and non price terms of loans. There has to be parameters beyond which no proposes would be entertained. There may be separate rating frameworks for corporate and small borrowers. It has to be ensured that market risk exposures should be considered in the watching framework and risk assessment has to be reviewed periodically. The banks are expected to undertake comprehensive study on migration of borrowers in the ratings.

Credit risk rating facilitates in deciding the grade upto which additional exposure can be considered. Scientific systems to price the credit risk have to consider the expected probability of default. The higher the risk category, the volume of collateral required will be more and the along with the margins stipulated. There has to be a slight from availing credit facility through cash credit limit to term lending in working capital. Further, the delegation of loaning process may be linked to risk rating of a borrower. In low risk cases removal facilities may be of longer duration.

Any credit rating system has to comprise sensitivity of ratings to real charges in credit quality, has time with respect to recognized changes in quality and stability of ratings when no changes has accrued. The different risks to be considered one; financial risk (bench mark rationed financials, trend analysis and subjective assessment); Business risk (with reference to objective and subjective parameters as to success or failure factors); management risk (objective and subjective evaluation of management) and industry risk (industry rating based on various parameters).

The parameters under each risk category are identified and weightage assigned and risk grades of asset quality can be classified as: minimum risk, marginal risk, modest risk, average risk, marginally acceptable risk, early warning and likely non-performing asset. Review of risk rating has to be through monitoring regularly by scheduled reviews for groups of exposures and occasional review of a business credit rating assignment.

Ernst and Young through their risk universe model, categorize project risk into different areas in business environment, information, financial, operational, transaction and governance. The business environment determines risks associated with people and culture, market structures and state holders such as employee or communication risk. Information risk is associated with intellectual property and information management system and includes corporate espionage insufficient. In security and disaster recovery planning and inappropriate system scalability, the financial risk is associated with reporting (tax, accounting, regulatory and compliance), capital structure, markets commodity, interest rates and foreign exchange) and liquidity and credit risks such as cases management, hedging and collectability. In this way, operational risk is associated with production and distribution, marketing and selling and product and service development. It also includes risks involved in physical assets and legal risks related to legislative and regulatory obligation, contact and liability risks. The transaction risk is associated with divestitures (process valuation and selection) and mergers and acquisitions (post integration and due diligence). Governance risk highlights issues related to risk management, organizational structure, community stewardship, company reputation and strategy planning and development implementation and communication.

Market Risk

Market risk is associated with market structure, marketing and selling, market development and competition. The emergence of foreign banks with sophisticated marketing technology marks the position of the domestic banks shaky. The marketing problem may be in different products and services and nowadays IT based products have to be developed and marketed so as to maintain a steady clientele base. It may be easy to satisfy a customer but to ensure a loyal customer base requires stringent marketing strategies. The competition may be not only amongst the nationalized, private and foreign banks but also within the particular group. The fact that many banks have failed exemplifies the negative role of management especially in marketing. The recent cliché of 'cultivating the customer' becomes the hallmark of any marketing mechanism. The entry of multinational banks with their vigorous marketing techniques induces compliance risk. The recent banking and financial reforms have time and again highlighted the necessity to reduce the number of banks and increase the economies of scale through mergers. However, where mergers take place and size is increased, economies of scale may not result owing to management and governance risks.

Government securities will have to have a 5 per cent weight for market risks (currently zero risk). Risk weight on a government guaranteed advance should be the same as for other advances. Foreign exchange open credit limit risks have to be integrated into the calculation of risk weighted assets and will carry a 100 per cent risk weight. The minimum capital to risk assets ratio has been increasing to 10 per cent from the earlier 8 per cent. The central bank can increase this limit for individual banks depending on their risk projections. The nationalized banks can access the domestic or foreign capital market since subscription to bank capital funds cannot be regarded as a priority claim on budgetary resources.

Commitment to winning new business and new customers including outsourcing will be essential for market success. Economic and social harmony existing in the economy largely decide the nature of country risk which in turn will be a determinant of the long term performance of the economy. Since any investment either in production or marketing will depend upon risk and return, for given level of risk, higher the return, greater will be the level of investment; whereas for any given level of return, higher the risk, lower will be the level of investment. Since investment is prime mover of economic growth Dipietro and Sawney (2001) argue that greater the inequality in the distribution of income, greater will be the risk because of increased social discontent and other externalities. This alludes to the fact that varying investment levels in counteracting market risks will show differing performances amongst the banks. Where the risk levels are higher the banks' general investment behaviour will be constrained.

Competence and Governance

Effective risk management results in competitive success and sustainable growth, which are essential for capability buildings of the banks. What explains differential competitive success and growth is differential organizing competence (Foss and Mahnke 2000). Organizing competence means complicated problem solving and risk reducing procedures meetings to production and marketing methods. Competence is concerned with processes and lessons for strategy. The banks have to be production oriented and value transactions with knowledge building and knowledge utilization. Opportunism and other incentive conflicts become in important and banks became dynamic. When they adopt the exchange oriented and transactions cost based governance, the transactions becomes the units of analysis. In such an environment incentive conflicts become central and the incentives have to be structured and properly rights allocated such as to reduce the risks. Where the bank has to be efficient in production (competence) it has to be equally competent in exchange (governance). If the banks could anticipate changes in the bargaining power of the contracting partners (banks, customers and others). It can take actions to mitigate associated hazards. If the safeguards are not sufficient, vertical integration will be resorted to as a last plank. Governance inseparability arises when the relevant hazards cannot be anticipated; also when changes in scope technologies cannot be anticipated. If a bank anticipated that an activity might be moved from the market to its over hierarchy in the future, it can make provision for this move in its early contracts. A bank may provide a limited franchise period to augments (especially in universal banking) if it could anticipate the need to forward integrate in the future. As regards hazards arising evaluation to employees, vertical integration cannot be used as a safeguard even if increased employee bargaining power is foreseen. This is because the bank cannot establish full control rights over its employees. So when future hazards are difficult to anticipate the banks face governance inseparability risks associated with being locked into governance structure that is inefficient for a new or changed transaction. With these risks the banks may prefer to avoid contractual commitments so as to remain flexible. While Williamson (2000) argues that greater uncertainty because it increases the difficulty of using contracts for exchange, increases the likelihood of vertical integration. But increase in environmental uncertainty may induce the bank to go in for market-based governance and strategic alliances with this vertical integration.

The new accord to be implemented by the Basel Committee from 2005 comprises risk-based capital; risk based supervision and disclosure of risks to enhance market discipline. All these are mutually reinforcing and have to be implemented as a total package. A new accord is expected to develop a risk sensitive framework that will enable the banks to maintain strong capital standards and adept sound risk management systems. While the banks will be expected to arrive at the requirements of regulatory capital based on the perceived risks in asset portfolio, such perception is to be accomplished by the supervisors. Many countries have started to adopt risk based supervision, wherein the banks would encourage efficient risk management architecture, adopt risk focused internal audit, strengthen the management information system and set up compliance units. The Reserve Bank of India has to evolve a risk profile of each bank and the supervisory cycle will vary according to turns risk profile. Under the prompt corrective action framework, if the capital adequacy ratio is less than 9 per cent and upto 6 per cent , the Reserve Bank of India may take action like submission and implementation of capital installation plans, restrictions on expansion of risk weighted assets, paying off costly deposits, suspend dividend etc. If the CAR falls less then 6 per cent and upto 3 per cent , more stringent measures will be applied. It is the function of the supervisory body to assess the quality of management and adequacy of its policies and internal control systems. That is provision for credit base has to be in comformity with the norms.

The major components of risk are, risk identification, risk analysis, risk appraisal and risk management. The management techniques will include identification, selection and implementation of strategies to control risk. The banks have to analyze various risks focusing on technical aspects and identifying and evaluating the risk associated with hazardous activities and events. Hazard identification determines potential hazards (including moral hazards which may be emanating from information asymmetry) and conditions which may lead to adverse consequences. Risk assessment focuses on the description, measurement and quantification of risk. Risk evaluation utilizes comparisons and judgements to determine the magnitude and significance of business risk. In risk assessment, the probability and magnitude of risk is described, estimated and quantified. The risk involved in asset management has to focus on providing accurate estimation of quantified risk and quantified uncertainty. If the process associated with risk is well conceived, a single value analysis using best estimates as inputs for the variables may be employed so that the outcome becomes a best estimate. However, if quantification of uncertainty is to be made, many values would comprise the outcome. In the risk management process, the regulations decide where, to what degree and by what means an outcome can be controlled based on the probability and magnitude of its effects. The different stages involved will be option generation, option evaluation, option selection and option implementation and enforcement wherein the alternatives for managing risk are identified, compared and choice made to combat the problem.

In risk mitigation, the activity has to be clearly specified as to its implications on the banks' performance. It also requires that staff responsible for implementation have to be identified. According to Ernst and Young Risk Universe, risks associated with corporate governance are often overlooked. Once the risks are identified, the risk profile has to be established for quantifying and measuring it. Each of the high level risk can be brought down until all the stakeholders are satisfied that proper risks have been identified. The recent corporate collapses in the USA and elsewhere have necessitated effective risk management. Hence there is a move to integrate risk management with strategic planning. This involves what is called as risk budgeting wherein the finite risk resources are allocated optimally. This may be similar to asset allocation. This risk becomes part of the investment process at source not something addled on later. The client and the asset manager agree on the total amount of allowable risk (expressed in terms of under-performance) identify where that risk has to be expended and employ processes to identify and connect any overspend, looking at risk adjusted returns. The bank may set a risk budget and clients may allocate proportions of their capital on a risk budgeted basis. However, risk budgeting mechanism is still in its infancy.

The Basel guidelines and the Reserve Bank of India's periodical guidelines have enabled perception and identification of bank risks in a systematized way and combating them at different levels has been made possible. To the outside world, the non-performing assets alone would seem as a major risk arising out from this. There are other risks like losing customer confidence, the loss of potential customers, and the loss of potential competition, which may result in efficiency loss. Banking industry has a tendency to be categorized yet with cross border competition and hence units gating the risks and improving the effectiveness of economics of scale and scope alone would sustain their competence and governance.

3
INTERNATIONAL BANKING

Introduction

Financial system development can be evaluated by different means. The ratio of liquid liabilities of the financial intermediaries to GDP is M3 money supply divided by GDP and is the measure of the overall size of the formal financial system. If its size is positively related to the provision of financial services, this ratio becomes a good indicator of the provision of financial intermediary services. The quasi-liquid measure focuses on long term liabilities. The ratio of quasi-liquid liabilities to GDP is M3 minus M1 divided by GDP and subtracts narrow money from the liquid liability measure of financial intermediary size. If quasi-liquid measure is used instead of liquid liabilities, because M1 divided by GDP represents highly liquid bank deposits and may not be closely associated with efficient financial intermediation. Since liquid and quasi-liquid liabilities, which finance government deficits may not reflect the provision of efficient financial intermediary services; the ratio of domestic credit to private firms divided by GDP can be used to measure the efficiency. However, the problem could arise when the credit claims would include credit to public enterprises as well.

The ratio of liquid liabilities as a percentage of GDP decreased from 85.7 in 1990 to 78 per cent in 1999 and that of quasi-liquid liabilities from 69.1 per cent to 54 per cent for the world as whole. The decrease in the former in the case of high-income countries has been from 97.8 to 79.8 per cent and from 82.8 to 76.9 per cent for the latter. However for the low-income countries, liquid liabilities share has increased from 37.2 to 43.7 per cent and the increase in quasi-liquid liabilities has been from 22.3 to 29.1 per cent. In both, the middle income countries have had substantial gains in the terminal year. In the case of India, liquid liabilities as a percentage of GDP has increased from 43.2 in 1990 to 52.4 per cent in 1999 and that of quasi-liquid liabilities from 28.2 to 36.1 per cent. The ratio of bank liquid reserves to bank assets declined from 14.8 to 12.2 per cent during the period. Total domestic credit provided to private sector by financial intermediaries as a percentage of GDP has been around 50 for the world total of 101 per cent.

Banks have been major financial intermediaries and the level of banking development can be measured by the ratio of total claims of deposit money by banks to GDP. According to Demirguc-Kunt and Levine (1996), the total claims of deposit banks to GDP have been 1.31 for the world, Luxembourg, Japan, Austria, Switzerland having very high ratio of over 2.5. Countries like Argentina, Mexico, Nigeria, Venezuela and Zimbabwe have a ratio of less than 0.5. In India it was 0.68 indicating an average share.

The proportion of domestic credit provided by the banking section as percentage of GDP declined from 51.6 per cent in 1990 to 49.6 per cent in 1999 in India according to 2001 World Development Indicators. For the world as a whole, the proportion increased from 123.5 to 126.2 per cent. The increase was substantial in the case of high-income countries from 137.2 to 147.8 per cent. Whereas the low-income countries registered a decline from 44.7 to 43.3 per cent , the middle income countries showed an increase from 65 to 70.5 per cent. Austria, Belgium, China, France, Germany, Japan, Kuwait, Lebanon, Malaysia, The Netherlands, New Zealand, Nicaragua, Panama, Portugal, South Africa, Spain, Sweden, Switzerland, Thailand, United Kingdom and United States had a proportion of over 100 per cent. The proportion was less than 10 per cent in Angola, Benin, Cambodia, Lesotho, Malaysia, Mauritania, Mozambique, Niger, Sudan and Uganda. According to World Development Report 2003, the proportion of domestic credit provided by banking sector, as percentage of GDP has been 152.5 for the world as a whole in 2001. The proportion has been 172.1 in the high income, 49 per cent in the middle income and 46.2 per cent in the low-income countries. The proportion has been 53.8 per cent in India. Japan had a proportion of over 300 followed by Lebanon, Switzerland, United States and The Netherlands and others.

Banking Efficiency

Banking efficiency also called as spread indicates the difference between bank lending and borrowing rates. However this measure may not accurately capture banking efficiency because interest rate data may not accurately reflect borrowing and lending costs. The spread indicator will not provide accurate information on how banks effectively monitor firm managers nor will it capture government intervention. This indicator shows that banking systems of Switzerland, Canada and the United Kingdom were among the most efficient, whereas Argentina, Israel and Turkey had the least efficient banks according to Demirquc-Kunt and Levine. The difference was over 10 per cent in Jamaica, Malawi, Mongolia, Peru, Angola, Belarus, Uruguay and Zambia. In Switzerland it was 2.7 per cent ; so also in the United Kingdom and United States. In India the difference is 3 per cent.

In addition to the banks the ratio of assets of private non bank financial intermediaries to GDP (such as finance companies, mutual funds and brokerage houses) show that this indicator had large values in Sweden, Singapore, Korea and the United States where the proportion was over 50 per cent. Indonesia, Pakistan, Turkey and the Netherlands had very low values. Countries having substantial assets in private insurance companies and pension funds have been the Netherlands, United Kingdom and United States. The Philippines, Thailand and Pakistan had very low values.

Countries with universal banking, has distinct from the more segregated legal and regulatory impediments of the United States, may develop different combinations of financial intermediaries. However, the overall size of the financial system across countries with different financial structure may be similar, as may be the provision of financial services to investors. Countries with big financial system may have big banks but the correlation between financial system size and private insurance and pension companies is not strong.

The stock market size (market capitalization) and liquidity (total value traded divided by GDP) one positively correlated with all the indicators of financial intermediary development except the ratio of assets of private insurance and pension companies. Volatility is significantly negatively correlated with these indicators except the ratio of assets of private non-bank financial corporations. This means that countries with well developed financial intermediaries, large banks and large private insurance and pension companies will have less volatile stock markets. Further countries with stock markets that are internationally integrated trend to have larger financial systems and banks.

Bank interest spread indicating efficiency of banking system is effected by many variables like transaction costs, taxes, net return to savings and investment. Interest margins and banks profitability reflect determinates like banks characteristics, macro economic conditions, explicit and implicit bank taxation, deposit insurance regulation, overall financial structure and underlying legal and institutional indicators. A larger ratio of bank assets to GDP and a lower market concentration ratio reduce margins and profits (Demirguc-Kunt and Huizinga 1996). The efficiency can be measured by using both ex-anti and export spreads. The ex ante spread is the difference between the contractual rates charged on loans and rates paid on deposit. The ex post spread is the difference between banks actual interest revenue and their actual interest expenses. The ex post spread differs from the rate spread by the amount of loan defaults. The ex post spread is a better measure because it contends for the fact that banks with high yield, risky credits are likely to face more defaults. A problem with this is that the interest income and loan loss associated with a particular loan may materialize in different time periods.

To measure bank efficiency (Deminguc-Kunt and Huizinga 1996) net interest margin is to be considered. It is equal to a bank's net interest income divided by total assets. Profitability is a bank's before tax profits divided by total assets. It may also be measured by the return on equity as opposed to the return on assets. A bank with a higher equity ratio will have a higher return on assets and a lower return on equity than a bank with lower equity ratio. In some of the developing countries where banks spread with extremely low equity capital (supported by government guarantees) their return on equity may be inflated. In such cases unadjusted return on equity will be distractionary than using returns on assets.

$$\frac{BTA}{TA} = \frac{ATP}{TA} + \frac{TX}{TA}$$

Where ATP is after tax projects from the bank income statement, before tax projects divided by total assets further satisfies the following accounting identity.

$$\frac{BTA}{TA} = \frac{NIM}{TA} + \frac{NII}{TA} - \frac{OV}{TA} - \frac{LLP}{TA}$$

Where NII is non-interest income, OV overhead, and LLP is loan loss provisioning. NII/TA reflects the fact that many banks also engage in non banking activities, such as investment banking and brokerage services, OV/TA accounts for the banks entire overhead associated with all of its activities, and LLP/TA measures actual provisioning for had debts.

Reduction in the net interest margin can reflect a reduction in bank taxation or alternatively a higher loan default rate. While in the first case it will reflect improved functioning opposite will be the case under higher level of defaults The efficiency indicators highlight how bank customers and banks themselves are affected by these interest and profitability variables. The net interest margin shows how the spread determinants affect the combined welfare of deposits and lenders. The relationship between interest spreads and tax reveals the extent, which a bank is able to shift its tax, will forward to its deposits and lenders.

The net interest margin has been over 10 per cent in Costa Rica, Jamaica, Lithuania and Romania; over 5 per cent in most of the Latin American countries, Nigeria, Poland and Turkey; between 3.5 per cent in Australia, Denmark, India, The United States, Russia and South Africa and less than 3 per cent in Austria, Belgium, Canada, China, Egypt, France, Germany, Japan, Korea, Malaysia, United Kingdom and Singapore; It is less than 1 per cent in Luxembourg, Cyprus and negative in Zambia. As a percentage of net interest income, overhead income had a larger share along with loan loss provisions and net profits and taxes. In Japan the share of overhead income was 61.9 per cent followed by taxes 16.2 per cent) net profits (12.1 per cent) and loan loss provisions (10 per cent). In the United States the share of overhead income has been 47.6 per cent of net interest income followed by net profits (25.8), loan loss provisions (15.2 per cent) and taxes (12.5 per cent). In India net projects has the largest share at 50.2 followed by loan loss provision (19.3 per cent), over head income (18.2 per cent) and taxes (12.4 per cent) for a net interest margin 4 per cent. The proportion of non interest income has been over 10 per cent in Russia, over 5 per cent in Argentina, between 3.5 per cent in Turkey, Philippines, Cyprus and Ecuador and less than 2 per cent in many countries including, Austria, Canada, China, India, United States and Singapore. It was minus in Yemen and Chile.

As a percentage of total assets, overhead expenses has a share of 2 per cent while that of loan loss provision accounts for 0.7 per cent and taxes 0.6 per cent. The proportion of overhead was very high in Argentina, Brazil, Equator, Hungary, Nigeria, Peru and Venezuela and Russia. The proportion of taxes was over 1 per cent in Brazil, Nepal, Poland, Romania and Russia; In India its share is 0.6 per cent and in United States 0.4 per cent. The proportion of loan loss provision has been over 5 per cent in Costa Rica, 3.5 per cent in Romania, less than 2 per cent in Argentina, Brazil, Denmark, Mexico, Nigeria, Peru, Russia and Zambia; less than 1 per cent in Australia, Belgium, Canada, Germany, Japan (0.1). 0.7 per cent in U.K and USA and 0.2 per cent in Hong Kong and China. The proportion of net profit to total asset has been over 2 per cent in Colombia, India, Philippines, Romania, Russia, Sri Lanka and Venezuela; it was less than 1 per cent in Australia, Canada, Italy, Japan, Korea, Norway, U.K and United States.

Taxes as a share of net interest income show the explicit taxes that banks pay like corporate income taxes; the implicit taxation arises because of reserve and liquidity requirements and other institutions on lending coming through directed or subsidized credit policies, indirect forms of taxation lower the net interest income rather than the tax variables. The tax variable indicates about the considerable international variation in the explicit variation of commercial banks. Loan loss provisioning is a direct measure of differences in credit quality and inflects differences in provisioning regulations. Net profit as a residual reflects the extent, which the net interest margin translates into net-of-tax profitability.

Non interest income shows the importance of free-based series of bank in different countries. Banks in Eastern Europe primarily depend on fee- based operations. The overhead cost reflects variation in employment and wage levels. Over- head share in total assets has been less than 1 per cent for more developed countries (Japan and Luxembourg). It is higher in the United States (5.6 per cent).

Demirquc-Kunt and Huizinga sample had a net interest margin of 3.5 per cent for all the banks and of the net interest income, the share of overhead income (minus non-interest income) has been 43.1 per cent followed by loan loss provision (25.8 per cent), net profits (20.6 per cent) and taxes (11.5 per cent). The non- interest income has been 1.6 per cent of total assets. The proportion of overhead cost has been 3.2 per cent of total assets followed by net profits and loan loss provisions (0.8 per cent each) and taxes (0.3). Foreign banks had a lower interest margin and in their case the net profit and loan loss provision have a higher share than overhead income and taxes. The non-interest income has been the same for both foreign and domestic banks and over head taxes had a higher share in the case of domestic banks. The small banks had a better net margin with a larger share of overhead income. The proportion of overhead and other expenses has been higher in this. The lower middle income countries have the highest net margin (5.7 per cent) followed by upper middle income countries (4.1 per cent), low income countries (2.8 per cent) and higher income countries (2.6 per cent). Net profit share in interest income has been higher in low-income countries followed by upper middles, high and lower middle countries. The shares of non-interest income have been higher in the low and lower middle income countries than the rest. These countries had a higher tax ratio and also loan loss provisioning and net profits. The net interest income has been highest in Latin America and transaction economies and lowest in industrial economies. The share of overhead income has been very high in Africa and Latin America and very low in Asia and transition economies. The proportion of taxes has been higher in transition economies and Asia and lowest in Latin America and Middle East and North Africa. The proportion of loan loss provision has been higher in transition economies and industrial economies and lower in Africa and Asia. In net profits, Asia and Middle East and North Africa have a higher share while Africa and transition economies have a lower share. Africa and transition economies have a very high share of non-interest income while the industrial economies have the lowest. In total assets overhead cost is higher in Latin America and lower in Asia; transition economies have a higher share in taxes, loan loss provision and net profits while the industrial economies have the low share in all these variables.

True to Gurly and Shaw hypothesis that under low level of development the commercial banks will have a major role to play. As development proceeds, other financial intermediaries and especially stock markets will have an enhanced role to play. When market concentration of three major banks to total banking assets shows that in countries like India the ratio is very high at 0.9 or higher. In the developing countries the ratio is very low, 0.16 in the United States, 0.39 in the United Kingdom, 0.48 in Singapore, 0.21 in Japan, 0.45 in Australia and 0.17 in Korea. The share of bank assets to GDP (total assets of the deposit money banks) has been35 per cent in India; for the developed countries the proportion has been higher-77 per cent in the United Kingdom and 98 per cent in Singapore, 112 per cent in the United Kingdom and 98 per cent in Thailand. In China it is 80 per cent but only 48 per cent in the United States. The proportion of stock market capital to GDP has been over 1 in developed countries and only 38 per cent in India.

The major determinants of net interest margin or equity divided by lagged total assets, loans divided by total assets, non interest earning assets divided by total assets, customer and short term funding divided by total assets, overhead divided by total assets and foreign ownership. Macro economic variables like GDP per capita, growth rate, inflation rate, real interest rate, reserves, tax rate, deposit insurance, number of market concentration, stock market capitalization and legal and institutional indicators also have marked impact. The above factors also determine bank profitability. There has been a negative and significant co-efficient on non-interest earning assets as a share of total assets, but there is no significant relationship for before tax profits. The pressure of non-interest earning assets depresses net interest income and profitability more in developed countries. The sign on loans divided by total assets is positive in net interest margin and negative in before tax profits. At higher income levels this shows that bank lending activities become more profitable. The liability does not affect significantly net interest. Though it may lower and bank profitability. About a sixth of a banks over head cost is passed on to its depositors and lenders and is developed countries it is passed on to financial customers. This suggests the existence of more competitive conditions in banking markets be developed than in developing countries. Naturally higher overheads will eat into bank profits. The foreign banks seem to realize relatively high net interest margins and profitability relatively poor countries owing to their exemption from unfavourable domestic banking regulations and they would be applying superior banking techniques. The foreign banks in developed countries may be relatively unprofitable because their technological and efficiency advantages may be insignificant and they may also face informational disadvantages. Per capital GDP has insignificant impact on net realized margin though it may have save impact on bank profitability. The real interest rate has positive impact on both margin and profitability.

Banks may face direct taxation through corporation income tax and indirect taxation through reserve requirements. Since official reserves are recommunicated at less than market rates, are proportions to the volume of deposit taking and is therefore a disturbing tax. Corporate income tax may be targeted at pure profits and hence may be non-distorting. In this way it may be superior to the reserve tax. Also the severity of the reserve tax depends on the opportunity cost of holding reserves. Under renumerated reserves lower banks net interest income and profitability. The bank may meet the full cost of reserves or may pass on to the customers in the forms of higher interest margins. On the whole it can be said that the corporate interest tax is passed on to the banks customers and hence may be considered as a non-distorting tax on bank profits. Further, it is a source based to on domestically employed capital resources. A complete pass through of this tax is consistent with the assumption that international investor's demand a net of tax return on capital invested in a country independent of its source based taxes. Deposit insurance has negative impact on net interest margins and profitability. While bank concentration ratio has a significant and positive impact on profitability, bank size has a significant and positive impact on interest margins. The existence of a charge stock market enables banks to have higher interest margins, complementing between debt and equity finance. As stock markets develop, better availability of impression increases the poor of potential borrowers into the banks. As the volume of bank business increases higher margins became possible. Greater contract enforcement requires lower interest margins and lower profitability in the absence of additional risk. A low degree of government corruption may be associated with lower realized interest rates requiring a lower risk premium on their investments. Where banking assets constitute a longer portion of GDP, the interest margin and profitability levels are lower. Government regulations such as deposit insurance schemes have an impact on bank margins.

Global Trends in Banking

Globalization has facilitated consolidation of bank margins. Financial deregulation and favourable legal and regulatory environment have facilitated consideration amongst the banks. The growing importance of internal governance, official oversight and market discipline has enhanced competition. The introduction of the Gramm-Leech-Bliley bill in the US has allowed banks, insurance companies and brokerage houses merge. The Citigroup has seen a merger among Citibank, Travelers Group Insurance and Salomon Smith Barney. The number of banks in the US has declined by 40 per cent since 1980. In Europe also the number of banks has declined by 25 per cent since 1985.

The consolidation process has been accelerated due to customer demands for integrated financial services and increased shareholder pressure to enhance value. Thus consolidation has resulted in decrease in the number of banks and creation of large and complex financial intermediaries. In this only relatively small banks can become efficient from an increase in size. Though there may be some revenue improvement, cost reduction has not taken place. Internet and e-commerce may influence consolidation through technology impact is subject to uncertainty. Since there may be a shift to risk asset, efficiency gains also become uncertain.

Another aspect of globalization has been convergence of activities owing to blurred distortion between banks and non-banks. Where universal banking has become the order of the day, bank assurance enable banks to sell insurance products while securities gives offer cash management services which compete with bank deposits (Swarnkar 2002). The need for a one stop engineering in branding services and integrating the multiple products with increasing size these general banks offer cheaper products and services aimed as customer satisfaction.

Bank globalization has enabled greater use of technology to reduce cost and improve efficiency. For example, the cost of a financial transaction done through a physical touch is $ 1.07 compared to $ 0.02 through the internet. Technology also enables better risk management and being about changes in distribution capacity and banks customer information through data mining. Globalization of financial markets has been achieved due to general agreement on trade in services of world trade organization and dismantling of regulatory barrier, use of communication and information technology and increased flow of capitals. The international financial market has become non-liquid and efficient through subject to market disturbances.

As a result of these factors global competition has been intensified. New entrants have entered, private institutions gaining upper hand by targeting specific segments in the value chain. Many mergers and acquisitions have taken place with squeeze in margin. This has resulted in certain circumstances poor institutions taking higher risks to protect their weekend base. Recent financial crisis has highlighted financial distress (contagion) being transmittal across the countries. The South East Asia crisis of 1996-97, the hasparado crisis in Latin America and the Russian crisis have been the recent fallout. The Basel Capital Accord to be implemented by 2005 is aimed at developing risk sensitive framework to enable the financial intermediaries to maintain strong capital standards and adept sound risk management systems. To qualify and for this, the banks have to assess their own capital requirements while supervision aiming at optimizing supervisory resources by focusing across of greater risk through explicit assessment of risks. This requires maintenance of confidence in the financial system, promoting public understanding, security of protection for customers and to reduce the extent of financial crime.

The international auditing standard (260) prescribed by the International Federation of Accountants required significant changes in accounting practices and could influence risk expanses. In the Internal Ratings based approach, the banks have the complete understanding of the risks they face and are responsible for their safety and soundness. Better corporate governance requires establishment of internal code of conduct and standards of appropriate behaviour, evolving corporate strategies to be communicated throughout the bank and by enforcing clear lines of responsibility and accountability. Establishment of strong internal control systems and risk management system with monitoring and auditing facilities become crucial for effective supervision.

Progress in Global Banking

A shift away from international banking to one of globalized banking during the last decade has changed the banking market significantly. Banks rather than taking deposits is one jurisdiction and lending in another could perceive the strategy of taking deposits and offering loan and mortgages within national markets through local presence. Some banks may perceive a capital market strategy wherein they may fund their portfolios of local securities locally as well. Thus banks are increasingly looking to serve customers through a local presence funded locally. The global or multinational bank differs from an international bank, which takes deposits in one country and makes loans in another.

The difference between these two types of banking is the way in which foreign assets of a bank are financed. The foreign assets are its claims on borrowers dominated outside the market in which the bank is headquarted. An international bank uses funds raised in its domestic market to finance its claims and borrowers in a foreign bank. But a global bank uses funds raised in a foreign market to finance its claims and borrowers in the same foreign market. Whereas an international bank concentrates on cross-border business, a global banks focus is on serving local markets locally. In the case of international banking for ex: funds are raised in the United States by taking deposits from US residents and then but to Japan (sometimes through a third country). In the case of global banking, funds are raised in Japan by the Japanese affiliate of a US bank and lent by the same affiliate to borrowers in Japan. Also, where the funds are raised abroad, the depositor rather than the bank loans the transfer risk. Global banks engage in cross border business along with their locally funded business. The importance of global banking may be obtained by comparing bank locally funded foreign assets to its total foreign (cross border and local) assets. The ratio of locally funded foreign assets to total foreign assets will be equal to one for a pure global bank and zero for a pure international bank. The bank for international settlements publishes consolidated banking statistics wherein locally funded claims may be weakened as the lesser of local claims and local liabilities looked by foreign affiliates of the bank. Banks contributing to the consolidated banking statistics report separately their local positions denominated in local currencies but not their local positions in all currencies. Because of this the shift from international to global banking cannot be measured precisely. Per countries with dollarized financial systems the consolidated statistics may underestimate the importance of global banking owing to lack of information about local positions in foreign currencies.

Cross border business (lending to developing countries) funded with Euro currency deposits had increased the foreign assets of the banks in the 60s and 70s. However during 80s and 90s locally funded business expanded more rapidly than cross border claims increased by 55 per cent to $548 billion between 1982 and 2002. Their local claims were mainly 400 per cent to $358 billion with a ratio of 0.7. In 1997 there was a break from the exclusion o derivative positions after which the ratio borrowed as the more broadly measured local claims have continued to grow faster than cross border claims.

Not only in the US banks elsewhere also expanded their local presence in foreign banking markets. Before 1999, the banks reported only their claims on countries outside the reputing area, mainly developing countries. In that year the BIS consolidated banking statistics extended to cover various foreign claims on call countries. According to this the US banking system has not become extraordinarily global. Canadian banks have a ratio of local claims in local currencies to international claims of 1.2 (in the US it was 0.83). This reflects the large funding case of their branch and subsidiary operations in the US from this it appears that the Canadian banks are as much regionalized and globalised. Spanish banks are also very global followed by United Kingdom and Switzerland, funding much of their foreign claims locally particularly in Latin America and Asia. The UK lead quartered banks are well represent in local markets not only in their Western Hemisphere but also in East Asia.

BIS reporting banks' local claims on Latin American countries increased sharply in the late eighties and is now as large as international claims. In the Asia Pacific region, local claims have approached the level of international claims and in North America the gap is closing; local claims are half as large as international claims on countries in Eastern Europe, the middle East and Africa, rising rapidly. Only reporting bank claims on Western Europe still take the form of cross border claims. When the focus is shifted from the balance sheets of banks incorporated in the BIS reporting area to overall international markets, it is found that foreign banks' share of the Latin American market is more than double that of any other market. Foreign banks' local claims share 50 per cent of domestic bank credit in Latin America; it is only 15 per cent in North America and Eastern Europe. The Asia-Pacific region and Western Europe have a ratio of less than 10 per cent.

If cross border lending is also considered, foreign banks have a higher share particularly in western Europe where cross border claims on large relative to domestic bank lending. BIS reporting banks have a much larger state in the Asia Pacific region than in Latin America. The balance between cross border and local claims in the above regions is somewhat similar. The BIS area banks play a larger role in Latin America than in Asia Pacific. While the scope for foreign banks to expand in Asia depends on economic growth and prospective market share gains, expansion is Latin America depends more on economic growth and financial deepening in the region.

The change from international to global banking indicates changes in strategies and constraints the banks have to face. The new strategies tend to lead in a balanced increase in local assets and liabilities. While the international departments of major banks spent the 80s renegotiating loans made before 1982, banks, which had made their name developing customer or securities business, improved their position. In consumer banking, the depositors were turned into the credit card user and mortgage customers and vice versa. Which led to balanced growth of assets and liabilities in foreign markets. The development of securities business within a country lead to a balance of assets and liabilities such as government bonds financed with repurchase transactions. The shift from holding to originating and selling international claims has reduced their cross border footing. The renegotiations of the 80s ended up in a new asset class for institutional investor bonds issued by governments and companies while international banks are holders and underwriters of such obligations the widening of investor base to include institutional investors has substituted for cross border bank loans. The debt crisis of 80s global over international banking especially in riskier markets. The foreign exchange prices led government to impose payments morotoriums on cross border loans. Locally funded, assets, subject to credit risk at such times, did not involve foreign exchange drain and hence were not affected by payment moratoriums.

Cross border mergers and acquisitions marked a record level of 8 per cent of world GDP in the late nineties according to UNCTAD. Financial sector liberalization enables foreign banks' expansion into local financial systems. In Canada restrictions on foreign branch banking and on the market shares of foreign subsidiaries made foreign banks to science customers from outside the country rather than through local affiliates. Financial crisis weakening the local banks often offers the foreign banks to expand their operations. Further decline of unremunerated reserve requirements as part of monetary control (as in India) also invites foreign participation.

In Europe where there are several important financial centres and inter bank money market is integrated has experienced mergers within countries and the introduction of Euro has accentuated the relative strength of international banking such that it has yet to realize a evolution in globalizes banking.

In the case of global lending there is a shift from transfer risk to the broader one of country risk. Transfer risk is the risk that the borrower is able to pay in domestic currency but is not permitted to exchange foreign currency to make the payment country risk is a broader concept covering both the risk of a change in the legal environment and that of changes in taxes within a country. Local deposit taking and leveling can avoid transfer risk but are susceptible to country risk.

In Europe where international banking is flourishing, in-country mergers have enhanced scale economies and amalgamation of banking and insurance. This has brought little change in its pattern of cross border banking. The introduction of the Euro has caused Trans-European competition in the loan market founded with home market deposits. In East Asia, the shift to global banking is partly due to the recent financial crisis. East Asia is not generally accumulating net international liabilities and hence foreign banks may not have an expanded role. China has opened its banking market (per pro WTO) including local currency business to foreign banks.

Banking in Asia

Customers have started seeking financial services to land to their specific needs in the profitable banking products but few local banks have the skills to maintain a lead. (Sherman and Wanders 2002). These banks have to follow the path taken by advanced financial institutions and manage individual customers, customer segments, products and channels specific to them. In spite of the financial crisis and global economics slow down, market for personnel financial services in Asia is satisfactory. McKinsey interviewed 400 middle and upper income households in China, India and other Asian markets about their views on personal financial services during 1998-2001. According to that survey holdings of financial products have increased. The coverage high income Asian consumer owned 3.2 of them in 2001 up from 2.7 in 1998. This however is only half the number held by comparable consumers in the US. People are willing to borrow and search for higher investment returns. There has been a shift toward more profitable transactions like credit cards, life insurance and equities. For ex. In Taiwan 62 per cent of households used credit cards in d2001 up from 44 per cent in 1998. Half of the users do not pay off their balances at the end of the month and spend up to three times as much on their cards. In Hong Kong, Aeon's offer of a 30 minute credit approval for affinity cards is quite popular even through they bean higher interest rates.

In China, the percentage of personal households and liabilities held in low yielding and savings account fell from 86 per cent in 1999 to 78 per cent in 2000. The consumers moved their funds into securities and increased the use of debt. In the United States only 13 per cent of household assets were kept in low yield accounts in 2000. However, many affluent customers seem to be dissatisfied with banks. About 94 per cent of local currency savings accounts are held at the primary bank, but only 50 per cent of the profitable credit cards, 33 per cent of mortgages, 25 per cent of the insecure personal and car loans and 15 per cent of less of pensions, life insurance and mutual fund. Therefore the local banks have to improve their marketing skills in this profitable products. It is common in North America and Europe to invest in expensive systems that can bundle much micro segmentation and sophisticated customer relationships. The Asian banks also are abandoning the one-size-fits-all approach and have begun to target specific market segments with Thailand services. Sherman and Wanders categorize the Asian middle and upper income customers as simplifies, advice seeks, self-directed planners, pickled shoppers. The simplifiers dislike the complexities of modern finance and want it to be plain. Their favourites are basic savings products, one-stop shopping, and face to face contact with low risk. Being older, less advantaged and less affluent these one the least users of bank services and segment and the simplifiers will not opt for high risk or more diversified products.

The advise seekers prefer one stop shopping but unlike the simplifies all higher receptive to advise and to more of sophisticated products. They hold the greatest numbers of products are willing to pay for advice and are the most open to using foreign banks. They are sensitive to price and conduct largest number of transactions making them expensive to serve. Professionals dominate the class and affluent that is natural customers for international banks with a local presence and for the well-established top tier local banks.

The self-directed planners are open to remote sales assistance (internet) and do not demand live service. They think they know better than the providers how to interpret information and want access to it rather than advice they use bank services pertinently have sophisticated portfolios, are investment oriented and accept reasonable risks. Such customers are a natural market for product specialists like fidelity a mutual fund company that uses remote channels as well retail branches to deal with customers.

Fickle shoppers have accounts in several banks and are little for advice with less money to invest and in more need to cash then in other segments they wanted plain transaction credit and product. While they may like face to face service help they may rely on ATMs or telephones for that. Unlike simplifiers, they are dissatisfied with their current banks. The shop accounts for the financial institutions to make money from these customers. A bank with a narrow product range and a network of branches offering basic services can concentrate on simplifiers on fickle shoppers. But a bank that develops more sophisticated products may target advice seekers and directed planners by using a slim branch network, remote channels and for advice seekers face to face contact. The banks can choose to tailor their offerings to different segments depending on their capabilities and growth ambitions.

In the focused approach the bank has to reshape its frontline force to suit its close segment. If a bank decides to focus on simplifiers because it can serve this segment most profitably with it is existing skills and assets. By contrast if the focus is on self-directed planning the bank requires a lack office extensive enough to provide many product options and also a more sophisticated font office to deliver information. Well-trained and knowledgeable front line staffers good for advice seekers may be uneconomical and offering to serve simplifies. The Standard Bank of South Africa has employed this approach in targeting urban low income customers and offering basic savings accounts, debit cards and personal loans and other products that appeal to low income people. The bank's branch and ATMs are efficient and simple to use wherein customers can open accounts and get cards issued rapidly. ATMs have pictures on the screen and branches are located in high traffic venues. It has two ATMs and two or three assistants to train customers to use them. Each striped down branch supports to 10,000 customers and the cost is usually 30 to 40 per cent below of those of traditional branches because it needs fewer employees to operate and uses more ATMs. The bank attracted more train 2.5 million customers in 5 years and is recently adding 50,000 of them in a month. Although the balances are relatively low the bank achieves a net positive contribution on the overage account because it has succeeded in focusing on one segment and in offering these customers only the basic streamlined services they actually want. Action which targets fickle shoppers with its credit and uses a similar approach now on while expatiate financial services attracts advice seekers in Malaysia.

In its two branch-one system approach, the bank serves a range of segments from a common bank office using various channels like travels, ATMs and sales agents to cater to the needs of each segment. In 1998, DBS Bank in Singapore acquired the Post Office Savings Bank Account along with its vast customer base. It now maintains two networks of branches and ATMs. One bears the century old Post office Savings Bank name and concentrates on the low cost services-cash deposits, bill payments and housing loans that simplifies and fickle shoppers want. The other bears the DBS brand and offers a broader ranges of services along with online and telephone banking that appeal to advice seekers and self-directed planners. However DBS and POSB products are processed through the same service centre. The two branch-one system approach depends on entrancing the strengths of branches, not entry blurring the distinction between them. A bank can create separate units with distinct brands such as Banco Comercial, a Portuguese bank based in Lisbon has ten brands each aimed at different customer group. NovaRede for example offers banking transactions to mass markets, while Banco 7 targets affluent customers with direct channel. The two branch-one system model is more expensive that the focus model because it involves additional cost of making acquisitions on creating startups though a common back office may allow for some economies of scale.

It becomes problematic for a bank to surf many customer segments through the same front and back offices because it requires high skills in product branding to ensure that the product has a district identity in each segment. Huge involvement is required for developing products and also in marketing there such that the different brands attract distinct segments and do not degenerate into a multiplicity of confusing names for the same product. Also, the branch staff has to be highly trained to recognize the segment to which customers belong to and to direct them toward appropriability. When this umbrella approach works scale effects will make it profitable wherein the bank can push several kinds of customers through the same physical branch and process the products they buy through a single back office. Citibank uses this model in Asia and elsewhere. Though it uses the Citi name and blue logo for all segments there are distinct brand for each segment. The CitiGold channel for example is intended for individuals with assets of more than $ 100,000. In 2001 Citibank Asia made net profit of more than $ 7 million from its consumer banking, asset management and private banking operations, comparable to the profits of Citibanking in North America. The Asian banks have a tendency to move out of the one-size-fits-all to a focused approach; they can move over to two brands-one system or even the umbrella brand. The Asian banks have to segment their markets to serve best the chosen segment and to adopt an appropriate business system.

The proportion of short-term loans in the 1990s was the highest in Asia, reflecting the rapid development of local and off shore banking systems and interest rate arbitrage by international banks. The share of short term lending more from a lower level in Latin America, owing to the higher proportion of long term loans to public sector entities and the impact of earlier rescheduling agreements. It may be pointed out that according to 1988 Basel Capital Accord, short term lending to developing countries was engaged. Under that Accord, international bank claims of upto one year to non-OECD countries carry a 20 per cent risk weight for capital adequacy purposes while longer-term loans carry a 100 per cent weight. The expansion in Asia and Latin America was due to the factor that the European banks want to diversify away from regions of their traditional players like Africa, Eastern Europe and Middle East and also because of growth of foreign direct investment and trade (Jeanneau and Micu 2002).

The North American banks were weakened by problem loans to Latin America in the 80s. The Mexican *tequila* crisis at the end of 1994 led to a major disposal of high yielding Mexican short-term government debt securities resulted in subdued lending by US banks. The US banks began to focus on areas where they had hitherto played a united role such as Asia, Africa, Eastern Europe and Middle East.

Although the stock of loans held by Japanese banks was large increasing upto the early 90s, their share of global bank claims declined thereafter. Mounting losses on domestic loans and pressures to boost capital ratios reduced their international lending. After 1994 they became more active especially in Asia. However, concerns about the strength of Japan's financial system shifted away from international business. With almost 80 per cent of their international loans being in Asia, Japanese banks had the largest exposure to Asia in any simple national group of banks.

The 1997 Asian financial crisis weakened international banking market. Though total lending to emerging markets peaked at the end of 1997, retrenchment was in motion. While banks moved to reduce their claims on Asian residents through non-renewal of short-term loans, they increased their exposure to Latin American and East European borrowers in the first half of 1998. However, from the second half of 1998, all regions saved Africa and Middle East were affected by retrenchment in international lending that followed the Russian debt moratorium. This reduced lending coupled with declining demand was noticeable in Asia where shift to current account surplus, corporate delivering and inflows of equity investment and external bank financing less necessary. On the whole lending activity has not recovered since in all the regions.

Bank lending had long been assumed to be most able than capital market financing, substituting for securities during periods of market stress. Owing to greater emphasis on long term economic fundamentals. The recent surge in capital flows has been due to changes in global macro economic conditions herding behaviour among lenders growing importance of securitization and institutionalizng of recipient countries, liberalization of capital account restrictions and financial sectors in emerging market economies and underprising of risk resulting from implicit or explicit government guarantees.

There has been a weak relationship though between real economic activity in major industrial economies and international bank lending. In a way declaration of economic activity in the main lending countries compelled banks to seek external lending outlets. As the slow down was associated with lower expected domestic returns was proxied by real short-term interest rates, which were declining. Under this circumstance, the banks had to seek higher returns through diversification of portfolios to higher yielding emerging market assets. Further international lending was affected by shifts in risk aversion in lending countries. Higher economic activity in emerging market countries was positively related to international bank lending because of improved consumption investment and trade and also favourable risk analysis, However, volatility of the nominal exchange role in borrowings countries had dampening effect on lending. A high foreign exchange exposure of banking systems in emerging economies increases their financial fragility. Also high levels of foreign debt in those countries led to a reduction in bank lending. The risk associated with these high levels refer to either the imposition of exchange rate controls or debt moratoriums or such of those socio -political risk associated with sovereign default. Investment strategies involving borrowing in a low interest rate currency and investing in a high interest rate are with a combined let of exchange rate stability resulted in carried trades, characteristic of tight exchange rate control. On the whole, it can be said that real GIP and real interest rates in lending countries exhibited a procyclical rather than a contra-cyclical influence on international bank lending. Stronger growth and higher short-term real interest rates in lending countries have been associated with larger lending growth. While fixed and tightly managed exchange rate regimes encourage bank lending; floating rates have an interlinking influence.

The terrorists' attacks in the US have had little impact on cross border inter-bank activity. Even though demand for dollar liquidity increased, dollar inter-bank claims stayed more or less unchanged. The Federal Reserve injected an unusually large volume of liquidity into the US banking system consequent on the attacks and the US owned banks channeled some of this liquidity to their own offices in Europe and offshore centres. However, these funds were not recycled through the international banking market. (Wooldridge 2002). The Japanese banks channeled dollar funds from Japan to their subsidiaries in the US, Swiss and other European banks, unwinding dollar positions vis a vis their own offices in the US. Dollar inflows from residents of the countries in which the banks are dominated picked up as maturing short-term dollar loans have not been renewed. The deterioration in current account position of the emerging economies resulted in net flows from banks. Their current account surplus halved to approximately 1 per cent of GDP in 2001 and may be negative in 2002. Slower export growth has undermined East Asia's surplus while falling oil prices in 2001 reduced surplus of the oil exporting countries. Declining interest rates in Europe and US contributed to the outflow from banks by reducing the relative attractiveness of foreign currency bank deposits.

Local versus Foreign Banks

As already pointed out, the share of foreign banks in India is around five percent at the aggregate level if assets, income and capital are considered. Before 1980s when most of the countries were closed, foreign bank entry was very much restricted. Nowadays it is common to find foreign bank branches in many countries, very much concentrated that too because of relaxation of restrictions. Once that established, the ultimate issue revolves around the relative efficiency of domestic versus foreign banks. For example, in the United States, domestic banks are more efficient than the foreign banks owing to linguistic or cultural barriers (Clare et al 2003). In developing countries on the other hand, the foreign banks may be more efficient tan their domestic counterparts owing to technical superiority. Cross-border consolidation due to economies of scale, good corporate finances system and governance and other natural factors. According to Barth et al (2001), the share of foreign banks in total banking asset control has been negligible in countries like Nigeria, Kuwait, India, Saudi Arabia and Iceland. The share has been less than 5 per cent in the USA, Germany, Italy, Greece and Egypt; 5 to 10 per cent in Russia, Switzerland, Finland, Indonesia, Bangladesh, Japan and South Africa; 10 to 20 per cent in Mexico, Malaysia, Australia, Brazil, Qatar, Philippines, Portugal and Spain; 20 to 40 per cent in Nepal, Venezuela, Chile, Lebanon, Poland, Maldives and Bhutan; 40 to 60 per cent in Ghana, Singapore, Argentina and Peru; 60 to 80 per cent in Gambia, Cambodia, Turkey, Zambia and Hungary and 80 to 100 per cent in Tonga, New Zealand, Luxembourg and Estonia. The share has increased by more than double over the past thirty years in many countries. Where foreign investment is high, the role of foreign banks also turns out to be high, necessitating closer economic integration between home and host countries (Clare et al 2003). While there are many benefits to be derived from the foreign banks like access to greater quantum of credit, efficiency in the financial system and others, there are risks involved like neglect of small and non-commercial borrowers and absence of credit availability during crises periods. However, it cannot be denied that because of foreign bank entry, the domestic banks tend to be more efficient.

Information and Financial System

A critical impediment to the efficient functioning of the financial system is asymmetric information wherein one party to a financial contract has much less accurate information than the other party (Mishkin 1997). A borrower who takes out a loan usually has much better information about the potential returns and risk associated with the investment finance than the lender. Adverse selection and moral hazard characteristics are generated because of asymmetric information. Adverse selection occurs before the transaction. This problem exists when the parties who are the most likely to produce an adverse or undesirable outcome one the most likely to be selected for a loan. Borrowers who went to take on big risks are likely to be the most eager to take out a loan because they know that they unlikely to pay it back. Since adverse selection makes it more likely that loans may be made to bad credit risks, lenders may decide not to make any loans even though there may be good credit risk. A problem occurs in debt and equity work its when lenders leave trouble determining whether a borrower is a good risk (good investment opportunities with low risk or a local risk poor investment opportunities with high risk). This is the situation a lender will only be willing to pay a price for securities that reflects the average quality of the firms-a piece below fair market value for high quality firms but above fair market value for low quality firms. Undervalued securities will not be sold in the market. Vender valued securities will not be sold in the market. Whereas low quality firms will be eager to sell them. Since asymmetric information prevents investors from determining the quality of firms, high quality firms will issue few securities and credit markets will not work since many projects with a positive present value will not be undertaken.

Moral hazard is an asymmetric information that occurs after the transaction. The lender is subjected to the hazard that the borrower has incentives to engage in activities that may be undesirable or immoral from the lender's view point with the least chance of paying it lack. Moral hazard occurs because the borrower has incentives to invest in high-risk projects and if the project is successful the borrower gets all the benefit but if it pays, the lender has to bear the loss. The borrower has incentives to misallocate funds for personal views or to undertake investment in unprofitable projects so as to increase his or her power or stature. The conflict between the borrower and the lender implies that many lenders would decide that they would not make loans so that lending and investment will be at suboptimal levels. Moral hazard can also occur if high enforcement costs make it too costly for the lender to prevent moral hazard even where the lender is fully informed about the borrowers activities.

Asymmetric Information and Banks

Securities markets are plagued with adverse selection problem wherein low quality films are more eager to issue securities rather than high quality firms. In this, private production and sale of information may reduce the level of asymmetric information but there is too little private initiative because of few rider problem wherein people who do not pay for information can take advantage of the information other people have paid for. If some investors acquire information that tells them which securities are undervalued and therefore they buy those securities while other investors who have not paid for this information may be able to buy the securities high along with the well-informed investors. If enough free riding investors can do this, the increased demand for the undervalued securities will bid up there low price. Because of this those who have acquired information will no longer be in a position to realize increase in the value of security arising from these additional information. Further it is less likely that securities markets will act to reduce incentives to engage in moral hazard. If some investors know that other securities holders are monitoring and enforcing the restrictive rules, they can free ride on the other securities holders monitoring and enforcement. This may induce the latter to stop their monitoring and enforcing activities. These results in not adequate resources are devoted to monitoring and enforcement, moral hazard being continued. Because of this securities markets become relatively unimportant source of external finance. That's why only the large and best-known firms in industrial countries issue security.

Banks have the advantage of reducing adverse selection and moral hazards in financial markets. They are subject to the free rider problem and can earn profit from the information they produce by making private loans that one not traded. It is bared to free ride off monitoring activities of the banks when they make private loans. Because the banks receive the benefits of monitoring they are in a better position to prevent moral hazard on the part of borrowers. The advantages in collecting information are increased by the ability of banks to enter into long-term relationships with customers and issue loans using times of credit. The ability to scrutinize the account balances provides the banks with an additional monitoring advantage. They can engage in low cost monitoring than individuals and can prevent risk taking by borrowers through threat of cutting of picture lending, thus reducing moral hazard. The greater difficulty of acquiring information on private firms in developing countries makes banks very important.

By adopting safety nets for depositors and imparting restrictions on bank asset holdings, capital requirement, disclosure requirements, chartering and bank examinations and prompt collective active, the banks may be able to reduce the problems of adverse selection and moral hazard. Where depositors lack information about the quality of private loans this may lead to bank panics. If there is no safety net for depositors and if some shock results in huge loan losses in 5 per cent of the banks, depositors are not in a position to know whether their bank is a good one or one of the 5 per cent of insolvent banks. Depositors at local and good banks alike have the risk of not getting lack the entire rupee value of their deposits and would prefer to withdraw them. Because of sequential service constant the depositors want to withdraw before the bank runs out of funds. The failure of one bank whether good or bad can hasten the failure of others. The government safety can short-circuit bank runs and bank panics. If depositors are fully insured there will be no haste in withdrawing the deposits because the entire deposit is insured against loss. Even where deposit insurance is sot formed, the central bank may play its lender of the last resort role and also guarantees that the depositors will receive their money in full. However, their own draw-back is moral hazard wherein the depositors may not impose the discipline of market place on banks by withdrawing deposits when they suspect bank deceits. This prompts the banks to take greater risks and at times the problem may be worsened. In such cases, adverse selection may take place wherein risk-loving people may play with banking to get away with fraud. If supervision is ineffective, greater risks will occur as happened in the US in 80s when big banks took all risks in loans which led to huge loan losses.

Bank regulations restrict asset holdings and impose capital requirements to prevent risk taking moral hazard. Bank regulation promotes diversification to reduce risk by limiting the volume of loans in particular categories. So regular bank examinations for monitoring capital complaints and restrictions on asset holdings limit moral hazard. Adherence to standard accounting principles and provision of information to assess the quality of portfolios and risk enables better monitoring of banks. The Euro Currency Standing Committee of the central banks of the Group of Ten countries has recommended that estimates of financial risk generated by firm's own internal risk management systems are adopted for public disclosure purposes. Sometimes, the regulatory process may not work as expected when the regulators and banks may not have sufficient resources or knowledge to do their job properly. In the US, deregulation of the savings and loan industry in the 80s prompted many entrants. From distinctive house mortgage loans, the institutions were allowed to leave 40 per cent of assets in commercial real estate loans, upto 30 per cent in consumer lending and upto 10 per cent in commercial loans and leases. About 10 per cent of assets were allowed to be in junk bonds or in direct investments. Many bank managers lacked the expertise to manage risk in these new lines of business. Because there was a rapid growth in new lending (such as real estate) rapid credit growth outstripped the information resources resulting in excessive risk taking. This created the necessity for expansion of regulation to monitor them. However, regulators retracted as federal savings and loan insurance corporations lacked the expertise and resources to monitor the new activities. All these things led to huge losses for taxpayers. In many cases the government had to bail out the banking industry not only in the US but also in Sweden, Norway and Finland and Japan which deregulated the financial markets in these countries during the same time.

A financial crisis is a non-linear disruption to financial markets in which adverse selection and moral hazard problems become much worse and the markets are not able to efficiently channel funds to economic agents having productive investment opportunities. The factors promoting financial crisis are increase in interest rate, increase in uncertainty, asset market effects in balance sheets and bank panics. When adverse selection lead to credit rationing, wherein some borrowers willing to pay higher interest rate are denied loans. A higher interest state may lead to greater adverse selection of increasing the likelihood of local credit risk. Though there may be excess demand for loans, market equilibrium will not take pace with increased interest rate because this will create a widening gap between restricted supply and demand. An increase in uncertainty owing to failure of some institution or recession or political instability or stock market crash makes it harder for the lenders to separate good from bad credit risks and makes information even more asymmetric which worsens the adverse selection problem. Deterioration in balance sheets negatively affects both adverse selection and moral hazard problems in financial markets. Collateral reduces the consequences of these problems because it reduces the lender losses in case of default. If a bank has a high network, that will have a similar role as that of collateral.

Asymmetric information is the source of bank panics and may result from problems in balance sheets, market crashes, unanticipated price and exchange rate changes and others. In the 19th and early 20th centuries, the US experienced financial crisis every 20 years or so. The crises began with a sharp rise in interest rates, stock market crash and an increase in uncertainty because of recession and failure of financial and non-financial companies. These increased adverse selection problems in credit markets while the decline in net worth due to stock market crash increased moral hazard problems which made it less attractive for lenders to lend resulted in a decline in investment and aggregate economic activity. The resulting bank panic and decline in the number of banks further increased the interest rates, reducing the amount of financial intermediation of banks. The spread between interest rates on low and high quality bonds considered indicating a worsening of economic contraction created by adverse selection and moral hazard. There were bank panics in 1857, 1884, 1890, 1893 and 1907. Once the bailing out of insolvent banks was completed economic recovery was possible. However, during the 1873 panic and also during the Great Depression, the economic downturn and contraction of money supply led to a sharp decline in prices. This unanticipated debt deflation short-circuited the recovery process and resulted in further deterioration of banks' networth owing to increased burden of indebtedness. Rather than starting with bank panics, most financial crisis began with a rise in interest rates, stock market crash and widening of the interest rate spread. Once a bank panic sets in, the resulting loss of liquidity causes interest rates to rise further, worsening the rotation. The Mexican financial crisis in 1994 occurred due to the deterioration of balance sheets of banks consequent on increasing loan losses. Deregulation of a financial system and rapid credit growth can be disastrous when banks and regulation lack resources to keep risk under check. When the Mexican banks were nationalized in 1982 they directed a large share of their lending to government. When they were privatized in early 90s, they had no formal monitoring of loans. Bank credit to private non-financial enterprises increased from 10 per cent of GDP in 1988 to more than 40 per cent of GDP in 1994. Thus when the banks and non-bank financial institutions expanded their loan activities, excessive risks occurred with many bad loans. In 1994, the inter-bank federal funds rate was increased in the US, which resulted in upward increase in Mexican interest rates. The central bank's actions in protecting the value of peso also contributed to this rise. The increase in interest rates increased adverse selection by making it more likely that those willing to take on the greatest risk would seek loans. Increased interest payments reduced the cash flow resulting in deterioration in balance sheets of households and firms. This increase was conjoined with increase in uncertainty in financial and stock markets. The Mexican economy was hit by political shocks in 1994, which further increased general uncertainty, and stock prices felt by more than 20 per cent , reducing the networth. Once the peso was brought under attack, the central bank's action toward a pegged exchange rate resulted in a substantial loss of foreign exchange reserve. When the government was not able to finance its debt with peso dominated bonds it increased issues of dollar dominated bonds. Increase in interest rates and fall in foreign exchange resulted in devaluation of peso during December 1994. The Peso value was halved by March 1995, which resulted in increase of both actual and expected rate of inflation. This further increased the interest rate and the stock market marked falling by more than 60 per cent in dollar terms. Since many firms had dollar dominated debts, peso depreciation resulted in a sharp increase in their indebtedness in pesos while the value of their assets remain unchanged. The asymmetric information problems were severe for both domestic and foreign lenders who had an additional burden of difficulty in obtaining information about the happenings in the economy quality pulled their funds out of Mexico. The real GDP growth fell from 4 per cent a year in second half of 1994 to around minus 10 per cent in the second and third quarters of 1995. Many firms and households were not able to repay their loans, which resulted in substantial loan losses for banks. The foreign currency denominated liabilities of banks increased from 116.4 billion pesos at the end of December 1993 to 213.9 billion pesos at the end of December 1994. The resultant mismatch between foreign currency denominated assets and liabilities on the balance sheet of borrowers forced them to default on their loans thereby converting the market risk for borrowers to a credit risk for banks with foreign currency denominated loans. Since these liabilities were of very short term, increase in their value led to liquidity problems. The government intervened to protect the depositors, thus averting a bank panic.

The central bank can promote recovery from a financial crisis by injecting liquidity through open market operation or through lending to the banks. The consequent increase in money supply increases the price level. This revelation lowers the debt burden thereby increasing networth. The prices of assets and stock also increased improving their network and reducing adverse selection.

In developing countries, expansionary monetary policy will result in inflation resulting in deterioration of balance sheets because their debt is denominated in foreign currency. Hence expansionary monetary policy and lender of the last resort role of central bank may not be the required succor to the developing countries as opposed to the advanced ones.

Effective regulation and supervision, proper accounting standards, disclosure requirements and prompt corrective action to stop the undesirable bank activities and even closing down banks not having adequate networth enables a healthy banking system. Financial liberalization becomes critical to the efficient functioning of financial markets. The developing countries have to improve their legal systems, duration of debt contracts and denominating debt in local currencies become crucial for the success of financial system.

In developed countries where securitization of financing is well advanced, ex ante as well ex post monitoring will be effective. Banks have the capacity to solve problems of borrowers by establishing information-based relationships. Government regulation in checking excessive risk taking in banks also enables reduction in problems arising from hidden information (adverse selection) and hidden action (moral hazard).

Because of banking crisis, Japan had to suffer a non performing loan loss of about US$ 400 billion (unofficial estimates 1 trillion) in 1995 which was over 10 per cent of GDP. In the early 1980s, Argentina suffered a loss of over 20 per cent of GDP while in Chile, it was between 13 to 42 per cent (Caprio.Jr and Klingebiel.1997). Government safety nets were not common before the 19th century and in many countries the central banks were formally instituted only in the 20th century. Widespread bank failures are common in the US since many states had unit banks. The lack of diversification made these banks susceptible to failure.

There are three types of bank insolvency- those limited to a single bank or a small member of banks, which are not systemic, overt banking systems runs and more silent form of a distress. A systemic run occurs when debt holders demand debt claims in cash to such an extent that banks suspend the convertibility. Overt runs happen suddenly and quickly. Financial distress of the banking system is relatively common in developing and transition economies. The distress can continue indefinitely and may progress into overt runs if the public doubts the validity of government guarantees. A systemic risk is due to a sudden and unexpected collapse of confidence with potentially large real economic effects. In this case, networth is completely eliminated; if loan losses are sufficient to wipe out capital then the problem is systemic. During the 80s capital in many banks in developing countries was less than 5 per cent of assets. If the non-performing loans net of provisions were 10 per cent of assets and if the collection rate was 50 per cent , the losses would completely eliminate the capital of the banks. If estimates of non-performing loans are biased downward the extent of systemic crisis may be limited. There were 86 banks insolvency in 69 countries, many in Africa, Latin America and in transition economies, a few in Asia including India and few developed countries, including UK, USA and Germany. These countries had experienced systemic capital exhaustion during the mid-70s to mid 90s. Rapid credit growth, volatility and shadow financial markets became harmful for growth of banking. The major reason for bank failure has been poor supervision and regulation, ineffective bank management, decline in the terms of trade, recession, political interference, connected lending, asset bubble, lending to government enterprises, fraud, Dutch disease, weak judiciary, bank runs and capital flight in order of importance. The measures to be adopted to deal with bank insolvency include financial deepening wherein broaden monetary aggregate as a percentage to GDP is increased along with development of real credit where; an increase in real deposit interest rate (if over 10 per cent leading to distress) and recurrent problems in the banking system after restructuring. The ratio of non-performing loans to total loans has to fall in the aftermath of crisis. Of the 86 insolvency cases, there were very few clear successes, 28 restructuring cases having mixed results and in many cases government had to tackle many fundamental problems.

The spread of bank problems and the difficulty of anticipating their outbreak reinforce the efficacy of monitoring improvement at both national and supranational levels. Banking crises arising from macroeconomic problems are associated with high credit to deposit ratio, higher foreign borrowing to deposit rate and high growth rates of credit crises stemming from government intervention are associated with high levels of government borrowing and central bank lending to the banking system. Those originating from microeconomic pressure however are not associated with abnormal behaviour. In emerging markets, capital and asset management efficiency and liability are not good signals for bank strength and more information is required regarding deposit interest rate, the spread between lending and deposit rate, credit growth rate and growth rate of inter-bank debt. These variables have to be measured against banking system average in which case it may be possible to identify systemic fragility. In developing countries obtaining this information would be difficult or may not be readily available. Added to the above variables, changes in real interest rate, equity price and money multiplier could be included. Such of those indicators which cross the threshold at a given point of time or a weighted variant of that index in which each indictor is weighted by its signal-to-response ratio, so that, more informative indicators will have a greater weight. If the available information is used optimally, sample forecasting errors can be minimized. Low GDP growth, high real interest rate, high inflation, strong growth of bank credit in the past and a high ratio of broad money to reserves are associated with a high probability of fragility. In this, exchange rate depreciation, terms of trade, fiscal surplus and GDP per capita are not significant (Demirguc-Kunt and Detragiache 2000). The probability of crisis has been over 50 per cent in Panama, Israel, Mexico, Turkey and Venezuela, less than 5 per cent in Italy, Mali, Nepal, Norway, Philippines and Thailand; between 5-10 per cent in Finland, India, Malaysia, Mexico and Portugal. Financial sector variables played a less important role in explaining the overall increase in probability, slightly offsetting the impact of macro economic variables. According to them the estimated probabilities of crisis was relatively low for five Asia countries (Indonesia, Malaysia, Philippines, Korea and Thailand) because these countries had very good macro economic performance upto 1996. Jamaica had a higher probability of crisis, which was because of high real interest rate and high inflation. In 1997, the bank fragility in Thailand was due to high real interest rate and strong past credit growth. In Philippines, though the real interest was lower than in Thailand, high growth rate in credit caused the fragility. Indonesia's high rate of inflation caused bank fragility after 1997. After that year exchange rate depreciation affected fragility in all the five countries.

4
BANKING PERFORMANCE INDICATORS

Introduction

There has been a rejuveration of the status of commercial banks in financial sector assets and liabilities in recent years. During the 80s, the share of bank deposits in the annual increase in total household financial assets has declined from 45.8 per cent in 1980-81 to 32 per cent 1990-91. In 2000-01, the addition to gross household assets in the form of bank assets had reached 41.3 per cent. This was because of failure of primary capital markets, institutions like mutual funds and non-banking companies. Further, there has been a slowdown in the term financing and investment institutions. Financial assets of bank accounted for 73.8 per cent of total assets of financing and investment institutions and banks in 1981 slipping to 65.5 per cent in 1991 and to 62.9 per cent in 1998. During 2000-01, the ratio has slightly increased to 66 per cent (EPW RF2002). However, the absence of expansion of credit use regionally, functionally and by the size of borrowers continues to hinder investment growth. Further, banks have not been able to deliver new forms of credit including project finance.

The various banking sector reforms undertaken so far have strengthened the stability of the banking industry. Not only diversified banking system resulted there has been a growth in other financial intermediaries like mutual funds, leasing, leasing finance companies, hire purchase and others. While financial regulation has been liberalized prudential regulations have been prioritized. Deregulation of interest rates has enabled the banks to determine deposit and lending rates themselves. Increase in autonomy, restoration of net worth by waiving off capital base and improvement in future profitability etc, have been highlighted. Broadening the ownership base of public sector banks has enabled private shareholders to increase their share upto 43.7 per cent (as in the case of State Bank of India). Further, the banking system had witnessed greater levels of transparency and standards of disclosure. Along with banking sector development, the financial markets have also developed. There has been a considerable improvement in the profitability of banks measured in terms of operating and net profits. The ratio of net interest income to total assets has declined indicating an improvement in the intermediation process. During 1993-2001, asset portfolio and net non-performing loans as percentage of total assets have shown improvement. During this period the supervisory strategy underwent changes giving the move from capacity to transparency a sharp rise. According to RBI survey (1999), net interest income to total assets showed a decline and there was a convergence across all bank groups except the foreign ones. The declining in intermediation cost was due to the decline in the share of wage cost. There was an improvement in capital adequacy, asset quality and profit per employee (especially in the SBI group). There was a decline in overall efficiency during 1990-96 due to a decline in technical efficiency both pure and real which was not offset by improvement in allocating efficiency. All this was due to poor performance by four nationalized banks. According to Bank of International Settlements (1999) data, return on assets, (profit before tax) ranged from -0.08 to 1.07 per cent in the Euro area. In 1998 while the return in UK was higher at 1.19 it was -0.74 in Japan. After deregulation, improvement in profitability in recent years is due to decline in spread which has been offset by a decline in intermediation cost and by a decline in provisions and contingencies as the level of NPAs came down. The decline in spreads has been contained because of decline in disintermediation. When companies are unable to use capital market as an alternative to banks, the downward pressure on loan yields may be less. Bank deposits as a proportion of GDP have increased from 40.3 per cent of GDP in 1990-91 to 41.7 per cent in 1999-2000. A decline in the ratio of shares and debentures in saving of the household sector from 14.3 per cent in 1990-91 to 2.5 per cent in 1998-99 indicates the decline in this intermediation and poor performance of capital market. In the first two years of deregulation, the profitability of PSBs was strained by new accounting and prudential norms. The private and foreign banks had no such problems. PSBs fared better in net interest income to total income (spread) over the private sector banks during 1994-95 to 1999-2000. In net profit, intermediation cost and NPAs, PSB performance was inferior to that of private and foreign banks. Since private sector banks include new banks also they will have a low NPA component. The old private sector banks have higher profitability and lower intermediation cost whereas the PSBs perform well in interest spread.

High interest margins have persisted in spite of financial liberalization in many countries. The spread is relatively lower in developed countries and in the developing countries also where prudential regulations are in vogue, there has been a tendency for decrease in the spread. When spreads are too large, financial disintermediation may take place and it may discourage potential savers with too low returns on deposits thus reducing investment opportunities. Where higher spreads are common, they may be due to high operating cost, financial taxation, lack of competition and high inflation rates. In many sub-Saharan African countries, the range of financial products is limited whereas the spreads were wide with inadequate capital adequacy and high share of NPAs. Where deposit insurance mechanism exists high reserve requirements may not be required. However, if credit controls are removed during financial liberalization, the quality of loans may suffer leading to systemic crisis.

It may be that the cost of poor quality loan is shifted to the customers through higher spreads. Further in developing countries, high non-financial cost result in wide interemediation spread. There is a positive relation between net interest margin and overhead cost. The cost of high regulatory capital ratios has to be covered through widening the spread. The extent of spread also depends on non-interest income. Banks with low non-interest income would try to increase fee income through sale of derivative products while banks with high non-interest income would try to lock in the spreads by using derivatives to hedge. This suggests a negative relationship between spreads and non-interest income. Further inflation is positively associated with spreads especially when the inflation rates on high and variable. There is a positive relation between provisions and contingencies (to total assets) and spread meaning that banks would push the cost of NPAs to the customers. Non financial cost (ratio of operating cost to total assets) has a positive relationship with spread. Where the banks achieve economies of scale the spreads will fall as market shares will increase. A proportion of higher non-interest income indicates greater diversification of bank operations implying its negative relation with spread. In the pre liberalization period the public sector banks had enjoyed monopoly power in the financial market and had a wide spread. However the interest spread delivered after 1991-92 but picked up in 1995-96 from 1996-97 onwards when there has been a decline in the spread.

Banking Aggregates

With liberalization and operational freedom, the banks are expected to achieve better balance between assets and liabilities. In the pre liberalization period, aggregate deposits had registered an annual growth of between 14.9 (1997-88) to 20.3 per cent (1986-87). In 1981-82 the growth was 15 per cent and in 1988-89, 18.7 per cent. In the post liberalization period the growth rate of deposits managed from 12.1 per cent (1995-96) to 22.8 per cent (1994-95). In 1991-92 the growth was 19.9 per cent and in 15.8 per cent 1999-2000. The growth rate in the post liberalization period has not shown any increase when compared to the pre period. Demand deposits contributed 16.7 per cent of aggregate deposits in 1988-89 as against 19.2 per cent in 1981-82. During this period the growth is demand deposits varied between 5.3 per cent in 1987-88 to 24.9 per cent in 1984-85. The growth rate was 7.5 per cent in 1981-82 and 15.3 per cent in 1988-89. The major components of demand deposits are current and savings account. Current account deposits attract no interest whereas interest on savings accounts is fixed by the Reserve Bank of India. It can be seen that RBI continued to administer the interest rate on a savings accounts in the post period as well. The share of demand deposits of SCBs was 16.5 per cent of aggregate deposits in 1998-99 as against 19.5 per cent in 1991-92. The growth managed between 2.1 per cent in 1992-93 to 35.9 per cent in 1994-95. The growth was 35.8 per cent in 1991-92 and 14.5 per cent in 1998-99. When compared to the pre growth, the post growth has been lower.

The growth in time deposits was higher during the pre period than in the post period. The annual growth during the pre period was 17 per cent and it was 14 per cent in the post period. Interest rate adjustment was very frequent in the post period. According to the Report on Currency and Finance 1998-99, the pre period was characterized by regulated controls on interest rates, quantitative restrictions on credit force and a high level of preemption of resources year marked for the priority and government sectors. During the 80s administered interest rate structure and credit rationing was quite common. The share of credit of SCBs in aggregate deposits in 1981-82 has been 67.9 per cent , 60.5 per cent in 1988-89, 54.4 per cent in 1991-92, declining to 51.7 per cent in 1988-99. The annual growth in bank credit has been 17 per cent in 1981-82, 20.1 per cent in 1988-89, 8 per cent in 1991-92 and 13.8 per cent in 1998-99. The growth of credit is conditioned by lending rate of the banks. For March 1981 no minimum lending rate was fixed but a broad framework of interest rates was provided with fixed rates on certain types of advances and ceiling on others. From September 1990 onwards interest rates was linked to the size of the loan, the lapse being 6 reduced to 3 in April 1993. From October 1994 onwards lending rates were deregulated except of those of credit limit upto Rs. 2 lakh. For limits of over Rs. 2 lakh, minimum lending rates were abolished and the banks could fix its own lending rates for such limits. The lending rate for this category was not to exceed the prime lending rate from April 1998 onwards. In recent years there has been a decline in all types of interest rates. Immediately after deregulation in 1994-95 the growth was 287 per cent as against 8.2 per cent in the preceding year. However, growth rate shared down from 1995-96. Like in deposits growth in credit has also in steady in the post period.

The share of food credit which was high at 7.2 per cent of total credit in 1981-82 declined to 0.9 per cent in 1988-89, increasing to 3.7 per cent in 1991-92 and further to 4.6 per cent in 1998-99. The share of non-food credit to total banks credit increased from 92.8 per cent in 1981-82 to 99.1 per cent declining to 95.4 per cent in 1998-99. The decline in non-food credit during the recent years has been due to the periodical monetary policy of the RBI. The annual growth of total investment of SCBs was 14.8 per cent in 1981-82, 17.5 per cent in 1988-89, 20.2 per cent in 1991-92 and 16.4 per cent in 1998-99. The holding of government securities was 31.3 per cent of aggregate demand and time liabilities in 1998-99 as against 25.6 per cent in 1988-89. This shift has been because of capital adequacy norms according to which such investments were rated as zero risk.

The cash in bank ratio, which was 1.8 per cent of aggregate deposits in 1981-82, declined to 1.03 per cent in 1988-89, 0.87 per cent in 1991-92 and 0.61 per cent 1998-99. Because of the reforms an improvement in cash management is visible in the post liberalization period. The SCBs resort to borrowings from RBI to overcome liquidity constraints. Changes in assets and liabilities may create demand for funds and failure to save this would lead to liquidity vissitudes. The annual growth of borrowing from RBI has been 41.1 per cent in 1981-82, increasing to 101.2 per cent in 1988-89 and further to 632.7 per cent in 1998-99. The quantum of borrowings was lowest at Rs. 815 crore in 1982-83 increasing to Rs. 7415 crore in 1998-99.

Performance of Banks

The ranking of the banks is normally accomplished by using weights for different indicators chosen according to the subjective review of the evaluating agency. According to Das (2002), all the 17 nationalized banks have been sorted out in descending order from best to worst according to values of business, efficiency, safety and soundness and labour productivity aspects during 1999-2001. The number of times that a bank appears in different positions equals the number of indicators under each aspect. The business aspect has eleven indicators and hence each bank would appear 11 times in total across the 17 positions. Once weights are assigned in the descending order from best (17) worst (1). The sum of the number of times bank appears in the 17 ranks as weighted by the best to worst weights has been calculated to arrive at the final rankings. According to these rankings 2000-01, Corporation bank was the top most bank followed by Andhra Bank and Oriental Bank of Commerce. Between 1999 and 2001, 8 banks improved their ranks and 9 had declined in their rank points. In these two years there has been a decreasing competition owing to increasing coefficient of variation. In business aspect Punjab National bank was the top most bank followed by Bank of India and Union Bank of India. In this also there was declining competition and while 8 banks improved their ranks, the rest had shown a declining trend. In efficiency aspect, Corporation Bank the top most bank followed by Punjab national Bank and Oriental bank of Commerce. While 7 banks improved their ranks in the rest there was a fall. There has been increased competition amongst the banks in this aspect. In respect of safety and soundness aspect Andhra bank was the top most followed Oriental bank of Commerce and Corporation bank. While 6 banks improved their rank 6 others had a fall and while 5 maintained status quo. In terms of labour productivity Corporation Bank was the top most bank followed by Oriental Bank of Commerce, Andhra bank and Canara bank. While 7 banks improved their rank, 6 had a fall, status quo being maintained in the rest four. In this aspect there was an increased competition amongst the banks. The listed banks ranked higher than the unlisted ones.

The various business performance indicators include growth rate in deposits, investment, loans, net profit, care net profit and provisions and contingencies; credit deposit ratio, credit and investment to deposit ratio; and market share in deposits, loans and investment. There are 19 efficiency indicators return on net worth, return on asset, equity multiplier, asset utilization ratio, profit margin, proportion of interest and non interest income to assets, total interest expenses to total income, provisions and counting exigencies to total income, wages to total income, operating expenses to total income, net interest margin, burden, interest expenses on deposits and non deposits to total income, commission, exchange and brokerage income to assets, net profit from exchange to assets, interest and discount income from loans and bills to assets and interest income from investment to assets. The safety and soundness indicators include capital risk asset ratio, tier I capital ratio, net and gross NPA ratios, growth rate in contingent liabilities and these two total assets and ratio of loans to sensitive sector to net advances. The productivity indicators are business per employee, profit per employee and staff cost per average asset.

A bank's equity multiplier compares assets with equity and a large value indicate a large amount of debt financing related to equity. The multiplier measures financial leverage and represents both a profit and risk measurement. The multiplier affects banks profits because it has a multiplier impact on return on assets to determine the banks return on equity. It's a risk measure in that it reflects how many assets go into default before the banks become insolvent. The profit margin is net income divided by total income (both interest and non interest) and measures profit per rupee of total income. The asset utilization ratio is obtained by dividing total income by average assets and measures total income per rupee of assets. The return on equity will be obtained by multiplying profit margin with asset utilization and equity multiplier. Thus it is possible to have alternative measures of profitability like ROE, ROA and PM, all having the same numerator (net income) but different denominators.

During 1999-2000, Canara bank ranked first in business aspect followed by Punjab National Bank, Syndicate Bank, Oriental Bank of Commerce, Bank of Baroda, Bank of Maharashtra, Central Bank of India and others. In efficiency and soundness aspects, Corporation Bank had the first rank followed by Oriental Bank of Commerce having the second rank of both the aspects. Andhra Bank, Punjab National Bank, Syndicate Bank and Bank of Baroda in efficiency aspect and Andhra bank, Bank of Baroda, Syndicate bank and Union Bank of India in safety and Soundness aspect ranked the next. In labour productivity aspect it was Oriental Bank of Commerce followed by Corporation Bank, Bank of Baroda, Dena bank, Bank of India and Andhra and Canara Banks. During 2000-01, it was Punjab national Bank, which topped 38 in business performance, while it was Corporation Bank in efficiency and labour productivity and Andhra Bank in safety and soundness. Bank of India, Union Bank of India, Canara Bank and Andhra Bank in business, Punjab National Bank, Oriental Bank of Commerce, Syndicate bank and Canara Bank in efficiency, Oriental Bank of Commerce, Corporation Bank, Vijaya bank and Syndicate Bank in safety and soundness and Oriental Bank of Commerce, Canara and Andhra bank, Bank of Baroda and Union Bank of India in labour productivity had lower ranks in that order.

During 1999-2002, in all the four aspects Corporation bank had two first rank, one second rank and one ninth rank. Oriental Bank of Commerce had one first rank, two second rank and one fourth rank. Canara Bank had one first rank, one sixth rank, one eighth rank and one eleventh rank. Punjab national bank had pone second rank, one fourth rank, one eighth rank and one eleventh rank. Syndicate bank had one third rank, two fifth ranks and one fourth rank. Vijaya Bank had one rank in each of the 10th, 11th, 12th and 13th positions.

During 2000-01, Corporation bank had improved its position, two first, one third and one seventh rank in the four aspects. Oriental Bank of Commerce slided down to two second, one third and one tenth ranks. Canara bank had one 3rd, one 4th, one 5th and one 9th rank. While Punjab National Bank improved its position to one 1st, one 2nd, one 8th and one 15th rank. Syndicate Bank had one 4th, one 5th, one 8th and one 11th rank while Vijaya Bank had one 4th, one 7th and one 15th rank. Andhra Bank improved its position to one first, one third, one fifth and one sixth rank. The overall ranking when all the four aspects are considered gives the Oriental Bank of Commerce the 1st rank followed by Corporation Bank, Bank of Baroda, Andhra bank, Syndicate Bank, Punjab National Bank, Canara Bank and other in order of importance. The coefficient of variation was 42.7 per cent , which increased to 43.4 per cent in 2000-01 indicating a decreased competition amongst the banks. In that year Corporation bank topped the list followed by Andhra Bank, Oriental Bank of Commerce, Canara Bank, Union Bank of India, Punjab National Bank, Syndicate Bank and others in order of importance.

The Business India Survey in 2002 considered indicators like capital adequacy, resources deployed, asset quality, management efficiency, earnings quality and liquidity as evaluating the performance of different public sector, private and foreign banks. Capital adequacy is the bank's leverage calculated after assigning different risks to asse5ts. The banks have to have a capital adequacy ratio of minimum 8 per cent. Tier I capital includes equity capital and free reserves and tier. If comprises subordinated debt of 5.7 year tenure. A very high CAR indicates the lack of realization of full potential of capital. Ratios which have a baring on CAR are debt-equity ratio (outside liability to net worth) advances to assets (increase in deposit ratio), government securities to investment (lower the risk for higher ratio) and government securities to assets (increase in credit deposit ratio, investment being lower).

The ranking on resources deployed based on total assets. Related factors include liquid assets, (low yield), investment, advances, fixed assets and other assets. Net non-performing advances to net advances indicate the quality of assets and real worth. Banks makes provisions for NPAs as per income recognition norms. Many foreign banks doing business with very few clients have will NPA levels. Related indicators are advances to assets advances to growth, advances to yield and investment to assets, wherein an increase in ratio indicates less NPA problems.

The quality of management depends on credit deposit ratio in improving income, return on average networth and employee efficiency. (net profit and business per employee). In earnings quality banks are ranked based on profit after tax and provisions. Related indicators are earnings per share growth, (equity dilution), spread (net interest income to assets), other income to net interest income and net profit to total coverage assets. The more liquid the assets the better but on the deposit side larger the maturity the better. Liquid assets are cash and balances with RBI and balances with banks and money at call and short notice.

According to this Survey, State Bank of India in the public sector, HDFC bank in the private sector and Citibank in the foreign sector have top positions. The top 10 international banks in terms of market capitalization have been Citi group ($223 billion) Bank of America ($ 117 billion) HSBC holdings ($ 116 billion) wells Fargo ($ 90 billion), Royal Bank of Scotland ($ 83 billion), JP Morgan Chase ($72 billion), UBS (170 billion), Lloyds TSB group ($ 60 billion), Barclays bank ($ 57 billion) and Wachovia group ($52 billion).

The top 10 Indian Banks according to assets are topped by SBI ($74 billion) followed by ICICI bank ($ 22 billion), Punjab National Bank ($ 16 billion) Canara Bank, Bank of Baroda, and Bank of India ($ 15 billion each), Central Bank ($ 11 billion), Union Bank of India ($ 9 billion), Indian Overseas Bank ($ 8 billion) and Oriental Bank of Commerce ($ 7 billion). When the seven associates of SBI are considered the State Bank group will have an asset of $ 94 billion. This can be compared with the ten top global banks led by Mizuho holdings ($ 1178 billion), Citicorp ($ 1051 billion) Sumitomo Mitsui ($ 840 billion), Deutsche Bank ($ 809 billion), Mitsubishi Tokyo ($ 751 billion), UBS ($ 747 billion), HSBC holdings ($ 696 billion), JP Morgan Chase ($ 694 billion) and Hypovereins Bank ($ 642 billion).

In capital adequacy, OCBC bank has a CAR of 192 per cent followed by Toronto Dominion Bank (173 per cent) KBC bank (97 per cent) Corporation Bank (18 per cent) HDFC bank (13.9 per cent) Karnataka Bank (13 per cent) Vijaya Bank (12.3 per cent) Syndicate Bank (12.1 per cent), Canara Bank (11.9 per cent) ICICI Bank (11.6 per cent), SBI (11.1 per cent), HSBC (10.9) IDBI Bank (9.6 per cent) and Dena Bank (7.6 per cent). Indian bank (1.7 per cent) and Nedungadi Bank (-1.93 per cent) have very low CAR,

The Debt Equity Ratio has been around zero for very high CAR banks, 10 for Corporation bank, HDFC bank and UBI; more than 16 per cent in Karnataka and Canara banks and SBI and more than 20 per cent in Vijaya and Syndicate banks. The advance to asset ratio has been 44 per cent in Corporation, Karnataka, Canara and Oriental Bank of Commerce; less than 40 per cent in Vijaya Bank and over 45 per cent in Syndicate Bank. The proportion of government securities to investment has been 100 per cent in some of the foreign banks, over 70 per cent in Corporation, Karnataka, Vijaya, Syndicate and Canara Banks and SBI. Bank of Baroda has a ratio of only 60 per cent while Commerz Bank has a zero percentage. That bank has zero percentage in government securities to asset 100. The ratio has been over 30 per cent in most of the banks listed above and 22 per cent in Canara Banks.

Resources Deployed

State Bank of India has the largest asset amongst Indian banks at Rs. 3482.3 billion. Along with its associates at has an asset with Rs. 4495 billion. ICICI bank tops the private banks with Rs. 1041 billion. Punjab National Banks Canara Bank, Bank of Baroda and Bank of India has an asset of over 700 billion. The asset value has been Rs. 317.6 billion in Syndicate Bank, Rs. 242.9 billion in Corporation bank, HDFC bank Rs. 237.9 billion, Citibank Rs. 215 billion, Vijaya bank Rs. 161.4 billion, Karnataka Bank is Rs. 77.6 billion. At the bottom rung some of the foreign banks like OCS bank, Commerz Bank, and Krung Thai Bank have less than Rs. 1 billion. The liquid asset ratio has been over 10 per cent in HDFC, Vijaya, Canara, SBI, ICICI and other banks. The ratio is less than 10 in Syndicate Bank, Corporation bank and Karnataka bank. The advance to asset ratio has been over 45 per cent in Canara, ICICI, Syndicate and Bank of Baroda and less than that in SBI Vijaya, Corporation and other banks. The investment to asset ratio has been over 40 per cent in SBI, Corporation, Vijaya and Karnataka banks and less than 40 per cent in Canara and Syndicate banks. The proportion of fixed assets to total assets has been less than 1 per cent in SBI, Canara and Karnataka banks and over 1 per cent in Syndicate,

Corporation, and Vijaya banks. The proportion of other assets has been over 304 per cent in all the banks.

Asset Quality

The proportion of net NPA to net advances has been zero or less than 1 per cent in most of the foreign banks, 2.31 per cent in Corporation, 3.89 per cent in Canara, 4 per cent in Syndicate 4.7 per cent in ICICI, 5.66 per cent in SBI, 5.9 per cent in Karnataka, 6.02 per cent in Vijaya, 7.64 per cent in SBM, 11 per cent in Allahabad, 16.4 per cent in Dena, 36.04 per cent in Barclays and 100 per cent in Commerz Bank. The rate of growth of advance has been -100 per cent in Dresdner and KBC banks 16.6 per cent in Bank of America, 27.8 per cent in Corporation Bank, 19 per cent in Canara Bank, 13.5 per cent in Syndicate Bank, 56.9 per cent in ICICI bank, 6.4 per cent in SBI, 20.8 per cent in Karnataka and 8.3 per cent in Vijaya bank.

In advance to asset ratio, ICICI, Canara, Syndicate, Corporation and Karnataka banks have over 44 per cent while SBI and Vijaya bank have less than 40 per cent. The Dresdner and KSC banks have a zero percentage. The investment to asset ratio has been over 40 per cent in SBI, Corporation, Karnataka and Vijaya banks and around 38 per cent in Syndicate bank, 34 per cent in ICICI bank and 32 per cent in Canara bank.

The rate of yield on advances has been over 16 per cent in most of the banks and slightly less than 10 per cent in SBI. The rate of investment yield has been similar. Investment growth has been negative in Corporation bank, around 10 per cent in Canara and Syndicate banks and over 20 per cent in SBI, Karnataka and Vijaya banks.

Management Quality

The credit deposit ratio (total advances to total deposits) indicates management's aggressiveness to improve income. In OCBC bank, it is 640 per cent , 180 per cent in Development Bank of Singapore, 154 per cent in Bank of America and 76 per cent in Deutsche bank. It is very high amongst Indian private banks like ICICI bank (147 per cent), average in other banks-Corporation bank (59 per cent), Canara and Syndicate bank (52 per cent), Karnataka Bank (49 per cent), State Bank of India 45 per cent and Vijaya Bank 42 per cent. The return of average net worth is a prime indicator of management's capacity to provide adequate returns. The return is greater than 20 per cent in almost all the above banks except in SBI where it is 17 per cent. The net profit per employee has been over Rs. 40 lakh in some of the foreign banks, around Rs. 5 lakh in ICICI bank, around Rs3 lakh in Corporation bank, Rs. 2 lakh in Canara and Karnataka banks and Rs. 1 lakh in SBI and Vijaya bank. There are banks where the profit rate is minus, the Mizuho Bank having the highest profit per employee at Rs. 1181 lakh. When the advances and deposits are added together the business per employee has been over Rs. 2000 lakh in some of the foreign banks. The ICICI bank has Rs. 487 lakh, Corporation, Karnataka and Canara banks over Rs. 200 lakh in each while Vijaya, SBI and Syndicate banks have around Rs. 170 lakh. Based on these indicators the composite score of management quality shows that the foreign banks at the top. Amongst the Indian banks HDFC bank tops, followed by Corporation bank, Canara bank, Karnataka bank, ICICI bank, Vijaya bank, Syndicate bank and SBI in the order of importance. Dena bank; Indian bank and Nedungadi bank have very poor management quality.

Earning Quality

In net profit in absolute value SBI tops the list with Rs. 2432 crore followed by Canara bank (Rs. 741 crore), Punjab National Bank, Bank of Baroda and Bank of India (over Rs. 500 crore), Corporation bank (Rs. 373 crore), Citibank (Rs. 325 crore), HDFC bank (Rs. 297 crore), Vijaya bank (Rs. 131 crore) Karnataka bank (Rs. 91 crore) and IDBI bank (Rs. 52 crore), OCBC bank, Nedumgadi and Sonali banks had very low profits at less than Rs. 2 crore. Mizuho bank, Standchart Grindlays bank and Centurion bank have negative profit. The growth of earnings per share has been over 100 per cent in some of the banks like Canara Bank, Karnataka bank and Union bank of India. 99 per cent in Vijaya bank, 52 per cent in SBI, 19 per cent in Corporation Bank, 7 per cent in Syndicate bank and -52 per cent in Citibank. The interest spread has been over 2.6 per cent of income in most of the banks except in Karnataka bank where it was 1.8 per cent. The proportion of other income to net interest income has been over 60 per cent in Corporation and Canara banks and around 30 per cent in Vijaya and Syndicate banks. It was 97 per cent in ICICI bank and Citibank and 172 per cent in Karnataka bank and over 200 per cent in UTI bank. Net profit as a percentage to total average assets has been 1.26 per cent in Karnataka bank, 1.07 per cent in

Canara Bank, 0.73 per cent in SBI, 0.86 per cent in Vijaya Bank, 0.84 per cent in Syndicate Bank, 1.5 per cent in HDFC bank, 0.42 per cent ICICI bank and Citibank and 0.34 per cent in Corporation bank. There are banks like Centurion bank, which have a minus figure.

Liquidity

The proportion of liquid assets (cash and balance with RBI and other banks and money at call and short notice) to total assets have been very high in banks like OCBC bank (62.4 per cent). It is 18.7 per cent in SBI, 17.3 per cent in Canara Bank, 12.3 per cent in ICICI bank, 10.3 per cent in Vijaya bank, 9.9 per cent in Syndicate Bank, 8.9 per cent in Corporation Bank, 8.3 per cent in Karnataka bank and 5 per cent in Indian Bank. The proportion of government securities to total assets has been over 30 per cent in Karnataka, Corporation, Syndicate, Vijaya and SBI and around 22 per cent in ICICI and Canara Banks. The proportion of approved securities to total assets has been over 6 per cent in Vijaya bank and SBI, above 3 per cent in Canara Syndicate, Corporation and Karnataka banks and less than 1 per cent in ICICI, HDFC and many foreign banks.

Rating of Banks

The Basel Committee as banking supervision in 1999 has proposed a revised capital adequacy framework which uses (a) a minimum capital requirement pillar (b) a supervisory review pillar to ensure that bank's capital is aligned to its actual risk profile and (c) a market discipline pillar to enhance the role of market participants in ensuring that appropriate capital is held by prescribing greater disclosure. The revised framework placed had explicit emphasis on ratings. (RBI 2000). Risk differentiation between counterparties like governments, banks, corporates, and public sector enterprises or securities firms it ought to be done either on basis of external or internal ratings. The RBI favours greater reliance on internal ratings approach that could incorporate supplementary customer information and can extend to even unrated borrowers in the small sector. The banks in this process may be able to refine their risk assessment for better management. The necessity arises for mapping the bank grades into a series of regulatory risk weight baskets and development of capital change in the basis of rating grades while ensuring consistency between standard and internal approaches and having minimum standards and sound guidelines for the rating process. The RBI also feels that assessment may be made by the domestic rating agencies for assigning preferential risk weights for bank assets. This could enable the national supervisory authorities to have greater access to the quality of assessment sources and methodologies used. The new framework expects the supervisors to specify banks specific capital add-ones based on the risk profile of banks by increasing the Basel minima for riskier banks.

The recent Basel II capital accord has provoked concerns over systemic risk owing to model convergence and pro-cyclical lending. The banks in the developing countries will free competition from those of the developed ones as WTO's General Agreement on Trade in Services rolls out openness. The internal rating-based approach makes regulating capital requirements for credit risk to approximate the economic capital requirements. The large global banks may brook at lower capital requirements and transaction levels by cherry picking, best of deals by suitable pricing policies. This is true for acquiring AAA type of assets wherein the banks will release substantial capital by using sophisticated risk measurement techniques. However small banks (outside G10 may apply only simple risk measurement. Since the regulatory capital requirements will be high for the small banks, they may not final it worthwhile to compete with larger banks. The banks may indulge in capital targeting; deal pricing and performance measurement in risk adjusted framework. Economic capital will vary with the nature of risk. Through this market profile is to be pruned by allowing the shareholders to see their risk profile. The Basel II norms for complete implementation will take till 2006. Once the economic capital framework belongs to be restructured by them.

According to the new accord, which improved the 1988 capital requirements, scope for capital arbitrage and increased sophistication in the measurement and management of risk has been allowed. Under the capital pillar the current definition of capital and minimum requirement of 8 per cent of capital to risk weighted assets has been maintained. While the measurement of market risk process is maintained, credit risk capital calculation may be based on complexity operations. The standardized approach which can be adopted by less complex bank maintained the 1988 norms. But it expands the scale of risk weights and uses external credit ratings. Banks with advanced risk management can follow internal ratings-based approach with foundation and advanced variance. This may lead to multiple credit ratings of approved internal rating systems. The internally estimated probability of default, maturity of exposure and credit type will determine the risk weights. There will be a new explicit capital change on operational risk.

The supervisory pillar emphasizes development of sound internal procedures to access capital adequacy based on risk profile. The internal process will be subject to supervisory evaluation review and intervention. The third market pillar aims at improving market discipline through enhanced bank disclosures. When the accord is implemented the capital requirement will be high and the internal systems for assessment and management of risk has to be strengthened with improved internal control. This will also improve the skill of human resources and that of market

Efficiency in Indian Banks

Measurement of efficiency helps to distinguish between financial entities to rank their performance and also to assess their position with regard to the prudential norms. Efficiency could be technical and economic. Technical efficiency arises when a bank minimizes its inputs given the outputs while economic efficiency maximizes output given the inputs. Technical efficiency becomes input saving and economic efficiency is output augmenting. Economic efficiency involves technical efficiency but not vice versa. A study of banks is Norway. Sweden and Finland showed that bank is Sweden is most efficient. In a study on II OECD and 8 developed countries, the mean average efficiency was 0.82 with a range of 0.67 for Denmark to 0.98 to Japan. In another study of 427 banks in 8 developed countries, the mean efficiency value was 0.86 with a range of 0.55 for U.K to 0.95 for France. It may be difficult combinations of inputs and outputs given rise to different efficiency estimates. In working out the net rate of return the different portfolio combinations, risk and provisioning aspects have to be considered. In respect of technical efficiency, there is a large scope for improving it. The economies of scale in the banking sector imply an increasing operational efficiency in the banks. Studies on universal banking using efficiency techniques will enable to fix the degree of scale and scope economies toward organizational restructuring. Further the efficiency measures could be used to improve the predictive accuracy of forecasting the problems and improving a basis for improving efficiency. In the U.S, banks and savings and loan institutions with low efficiency failed at higher rates than institutions with higher efficiency.

The proportion of income to total assets for all commercial banks had delivered from 10.8 per cent to 10.4 per cent during the two years. The decline has been higher in the SBI group (10.7 to 10.1 per cent) while the nationalized banks had a more or less constant share at 10.3 per cent. The decline in income share has been notable in the new private banks are (11.7 per cent to 9.2 per cent) than in the old private banks (11.7 per cent to 11.3 per cent). The proportion of income has been higher in the case of foreign bank at 13.4 per cent of total asset in 1997-98 declining to 12.5 per cent in 1999-2000. Interest income accorded for 86 per cent of total income for all the banks in 1997-98 and the proportion remained more or less same in 1999-2000 indicating lack of diversification. The proportion was 853 per cent in the SBI Group increasing to 85.8 per cent in 1999-2000. For the nationalized banks the declining proportion has been around 88 per cent in both the years. For the old private banks there has been a slight decline from 85.3 to 85.0 per cent. In the case of new private banks the share showed an increase from 79 per cent to 82 per cent.

The proportion of expenditure to total assets slightly declined from 10 to 9.7 per cent for all the banks, the SBI group registering a decline from 9.6 per cent to 9.3 per cent while the nationalized banks registered an increase from 9.66 to 9.82 per cent. Because of this for the public sector banks the expenditure share remained constant at around 9.65 per cent. The decline in the old private bank has been from 10.9 to 10.4 per cent while the new private banks registered a significant saving from 10.1 to 8.2 per cent. The foreign banks had a higher share of expenditure at 12.4 per cent , declining to 11.3 per cent in 1999-2000.

There has been a slight decline in the proportion of operating expenses (2.63 to 2.49 per cent of assets). While the proportion has been around the average in the public sector banks it has been lower in the old private bank and much lower in the new private banks. The foreign banks had a higher share increasing from 2.97 to 3.2 per cent. The proportion of wage till also has declined from 1.77 to 1.66 per cent of assets for the banks, from 2.0 to 1.8 per cent in the SBI group, from 1.91 to 1.88 per cent in the nationalized banks, from 1.4 to 1.39 per cent in the old private banks while the share which was the lowest in the new private banks declined from 0.31 to 0.28 per cent. The proportion in the foreign banks is higher than the new private banks, but lower than the PSBs and old private banks at 0.95 per cent increasing to 1.04 per cent. In regard to provisions and contingencies the share remained more or less constant at 1 per cent , the PSBs having a lower share than in private and foreign banks. The net interest income (spread) slightly declined from 2.95 per cent to 2.72 per cent indicating an increase in efficiency and an increased dependence on non interest income. The spread has been higher in SBI group at 3.14 per cent , declining to 2.76 per cent while in the nationalized banks the decline has been from 2.78 to 2.67 per cent. The decline has been from 2.57 to 2.33 per cent for the old private banks and from 2.93 to 2.85 per cent for the foreign banks while the new private banks having a lower share have shown a decline from 2.23 to 1.87 per cent.

The proportion of operating profit as percentage of total assets has slightly declined from 1.69 per cent in 1995-96 to 1.66 per cent in 1999-2000 for all the commercial banks. The share has been higher for the private and foreign banks. The decline in the share of SBI group has been from 2.1 to 1.74 per cent while the nationalized banks increased their share from 1.14 to 1.3 per cent. The old private banks witnessed a decline from 2.1 to 1.84 per cent , while the decline has been from 2.77 to 2.11 per cent for the new private banks and from 3.35 to 3.24 per cent for the foreign banks, net profit as percentage of total assets increased from 0.16 in 1995-96 to 0.66 per cent in 1999-2000 for all the banks. The increase is substantial for the PSBs (from -0.36 to 0.44 per cent for the nationalized banks). There has been a decline in the case of old private banks from 1.06 to 0.84 per cent while it has been very high in the case of new private banks from 1.85 to 0.97 per cent ; in the foreign banks the decline has been from 1.58 to 1.17 per cent.

Non-Performing Assets

The proportion of NPAs declined from 14.4 per cent of total advances in 1998 to 12.8 per cent in 2000. NPAs consist of assets including substandard (not exceeding two years), doubtful (exceeding two years) and loss (when identified as such but not written off). The proportion of standard assets increased from 85.6 to 87.2 per cent during the period for all commercial banks. While the public sector banks had an increase from 84 to 86 per cent. In the private sector banks there has been a slight increase from 91.3 to 91.5 per cent , whereas in the case of foreign banks there has been a decline from 93.6 to 93.0 per cent. Of all the NPAs the proportion of doubtful assets has been more than 50 per cent followed by substandard assets and loss assets. The proportion of NPAs is the lowest in the case of new private banks (42 per cent in 2000) followed by foreign banks (7.0 per cent) old private banks (11.3 per cent) and PSBs (14.0 per cent).

In the NPAs, the share of priority sector has been 53.7 per cent in the SBI groups in 1995-96 and the share declined to 50.4 per cent in 1996-97, 48 per cent in 1997-98, 44.6 per cent in 1998-99 slightly increasing to 45.2 per cent in 1999-2000. In the case of priority sector NPAs that was 45.6 per cent in 1995-96 increases to 46.3 per cent in the succeeding year, slightly declining to 45.5 and -43.2 per cent in the succeeding years, again increasing in 1999-2000 to 44 per cent. This indicates that the proportion of non-priority sector NPAs has increased from 52.2 to 54.5 per cent during the period. The share of the public sector however declined from 3.6 to 2.0 per cent. There have been 5 PSBs which have an NPA share of 10 to 20.0 per cent in 2000, the member being 9.0 in 1997. In the case of old private banks the number has been five while one bank had more than 20 per cent. In the case of foreign banks the number has been 7 to 4 respectively. This gives the proportion of banks as having above 10 per cent NPA as 19 per cent in PSBs, 25 per cent in old private banks, 26 per cent in foreign banks and will in new private banks.

In capital to risk weighted assets ratio all the 8 SBI group banks have more than 10 per cent in both the years, whereas the proportion of nationalized banks has been 78 and 81 per cent respectively. The proportion has been 72 and 76 per cent in the case of old private banks 78 and 89 per cent in the case of new private banks and 65 and 88 per cent in the case of foreign banks. SBI with a share price of Rs. 291 has the highest net NPA at Rs. 6810 crore, followed by Bank of India (Rs. 2304 crore with a share price of Rs. 42), Bank of Baroda (Rs. 1913 crore, at a share price of Rs. 79), Punjab National Bank (Rs. 1810 crore with a share price of Rs. 81.4), Union Bank of India (Rs. 1338 crore with a share price of Rs. 25.8), Canara Bank (Rs. 1288 crore with a share price of Rs. 58.8), Dena Bank (Rs. 1227 crore with a share price of Rs. 16.4), Allahabad Bank (Rs. 1160 crore with a share price of Rs. 15.3), Indian Overseas Bank (Rs. 958 with a share price of Rs. 18) and Oriental Bank of Commerce (Rs. 454 with a share price of Rs. 62.2) during February 2002 according to Outlook money.

Credit Deposit Ratio

The credit deposit ratio of schedule commercial banks in 1997 as per sanction and utilization has been 56.8 per cent increasing to 57.1 per cent in 2000. The CDR has been higher in the southern region (74.5 per cent), Tamil Nadu leading with 97.3 per cent in 1997. The ratio declined to 65.8 per cent in 2000, Tamil Nadu also showing a decline to 88 per cent. In Karnataka ratio declined from 70.9 to 61.0 per cent. In the northern region the ratio increased from 48.4 to 58.0 per cent , Delhi registering the highest growth (58.6 to 76.9 per cent). In the western region the increase has been from 67.2 to 74.4 to 83.8 per cent). In the central region the CD ratio declined from 37.5 to 33.4 per cent , the declined in Madhya Pradesh being 52.5 to 49.2/ per cent. In the eastern region the decline has been from 42.8 to 36.8 per cent , it has been 45.2 per cent in West Bengal down from 50.8 per cent. The CDK has been the lowest in the northeastern region, especially in Arunachal Pradesh, Nagaland and Mehalaya. The decline for the region as a whole has been from 32.1 to 27.7 per cent and in Nagaland from 22.2 to 15.4 per cent. The CD ration in 2000 has been above 70 per cent in Delhi, Maharashtra and Tamil Nadu and below 20 per cent in Arunachal Pradesh, Meghalaya, Nagaland, Sikkim, Andaman, Daman and Lakshadweep.

Accounting Standards

Under corporate governance the banks have to articulate corporate values, codes of conduct and standards of appropriate behaviour. Further they are expected to have systems in control to ensure compliance with them. The Board sets the objectives and values and specifies lines of responsibility and accountability. There has to be a dynamic balance among the different corporate players. In this the ownership of the corporate sector and the structure of the Boards play crucial roles. In U.K, financial and non-financial corporations hold more than 60 per cent of issued equity. Whereas in Japan share holdings till recently were held mainly by individuals. In other countries the groupings are family controlled or industry based. The central bank has the responsibility on the nature of corporate governance in the banking sector, both public and private. The supervisory mechanism involves strengthening of the internal control and monitoring by focusing on identifiable parameters. Timeliness of information, interaction with market participants and appropriate functional and institutional approach to regulation demand transparency of banking operations. The transparency sub group of the Basel Committee on banking supervision identified six qualitative characteristics including comprehensiveness, relevance, timeliness, reliability, comparability and materiality. Comprehensiveness of information relates to the scope of activities covered by such information. Relevance distinguishes between facts from information and information has to be timely in order to be relevant. Reliability of information depends on its factual accuracy and freedom from bias in presentation. Information disclosed must be open to comparability, one for the reporting entities to distinguish between good and bad banks and it must be comparable across time to monitor the trends in the performance of the banks. Information is material if its omission of misstatement could change the assessment or decision of a user relying on that information. The disclosure norms relative to the pattern of assets and liabilities, foreign currency assets and liabilities and movements in provision accounts and NPAs.

The crises in the banking sector have necessitated proper and sound accounting standards. There have been systemic bank failures many countries. In Japan during the early 90s about 25 per cent of GDP was lost in the shape of non performing loans. In the early eighties the bank losses were estimated at 20-55 per cent of GDP in Argentina. While in Chile it was between 13-42 per cent. The episodes of insolvency have been caste by a mixture of bad luck, had policies and bad banking (Caprio and Klingbiel 1997). Before the 19th century there were no government safety nets and in many countries the central banks were formally instituted only in the 20th century. Widespread bank failures were common in the US because many states had unit banks with only one office. The lack of diversification made these banks susceptible to failure and the deposit insurance schemes could not provide adequate solvency.

Systemic bank insolvency drives resources out of the format financial sector and into less productive uses. This can also lead to destabilization programmes or retard the financial sector reforms.

A problem becomes systemic when the central bank thinks that an event would develop into a system wide problem. The insolvency may be limited to a single bank or a small number of banks, which clearly are not systemic, overt banking system runs and a more silent form of financial distress. A systemic run occurs when the debt holders suddenly demand that banks convert their debt claims into cash at par to such an extent that the banks suspend convertibility of debt into cash. Overt runs happen suddenly and end quickly. Financial distress is common in developing and transition economies where the runs are averted by explicit or implicit deposit insurance. The distress can per4sist for many years, overlooked by weak supervisory and regulatory systems and observed by the ability to make bad loans look good by granting new loans. The systemic risk is the likelihood of a sudden unexpected collapse of confidence in the system with significant economic impact when these crisis take place the entire net worth of the concerned banks may be completely eliminated. During the eighties capital in many developing countries was less than 5 per cent of assets. If net NPAs were to be 10 per cent and if banks collect 50 per cent on these loans, then the losses would eliminate the bank's capital. If the collection rate and capital ratio are higher, even a lower ratio of NPAs could undo capital. Caprio and Klingebiel present 86 episodes of bank insolvency in 69 countries. Systemic cases where most or all bank capital has been exhausted has taken place in many countries- Congo, Ghana, Kenya, Nigeria, Senegal, South Africa, Uganda, Zambia and many other African countries, Bangladesh, India, Nepal, Philippines, Sri Lanka, Thailand and Indonesia in Asia most of the Latin American countries and middle east and Transition economies have experienced especially in the 80s and 90s systemic crisis. Among the advanced economies Finland, Japan, Norway, Spain and Sweden have experienced major bank insolvencies. Borderline or small cases have been reported in many Asian countries and in Australia, France, Germany, New Zealand, United Kingdom and United States.

Banking crisis or a macro economic phenomenon and where the macro economic pressures as was during the Great Depression saw as many as 15,000 bank failures in the U.S but in Canada only one bank failed. Poor information markets and weak banks make credit crunch more likely in less developed economies especially after manor swings in relative prices. A macro economic shock or heavily concentrated loan port folio while lead to low or negative networth. This results in less incentive to manage the banks well and where the liability is limited there is the incentive to gamble or boot the bank. For example in the U.S losses in the savings and loan institutions increased from $ 30 to $ 150 billion between 1860 to 1970. Excessive credit growth has been a primary factor in a crisis especially in Latin American Countries. Volatility is another cause of crisis owing to large variation in output and prices, which makes it difficult to identify good borrowers. Banking crisis caused a part of the volatility in GDP and inflation. In 75 per cent of the crisis countries the terms of trade fell by more than 10 per cent in the years preceding the episode. Further shallow financial markets is often because the shocks may be more damaging and the means for studying their cause overtime are limited. Macro economic disturbances can weaken the non-financial sector and then show up in the portfolios of banks. Capital flight, Dutch disease, asset bubble, recession and terms of trade drop have been the major macro economic factors while the micro economic factors have been weak judiciary, bank runs, fraud, lending to state enterprises, connected lending, political interference, deficient bank management and poor supervision and regulation, the last three factors accounting for major share in insolvency. Wherever there is a bank failure government intervenes and cases of recapitalization in Indian banking system is well known.

The new reforms are intended to strengthen the regulation and supervision of banks so that the type of financial scams, which have taken place during the 90s, will not recover. A factor in quality management involves sound accounting practices, which would make manipulation difficult. In many countries accounting conventions for classifying bad assets has not performing are yet to be made tight to prevent banks from making bad loans look good by lending more money to trouble the borrowers. Distinguishing healthy from unhealthy banks is often hindered by the absence of financial statements on consolidated exposure of banks by the lack of uniform reporting requirement, by the lack of published key financial data on individual banks, by differences in accounting standards and by the absence of serious penalties for submitting inaccurate reports.

The result of many bank crises led to the necessity of sound accounting standards. The existing accounting system disclosure practices legal frameworks winder the operation of market discipline and effective supervision. It will be difficult to disciple the bad banks without timely, accurate, comprehensive and transparent information on their credit worthiness and also by their customers. Accounting procedures for classifying bad assets as non-performing may not be very strict so as to prevent the banks from making bad loans look good by lending more money to troubled borrowers. Distinguishing healthy from unhealthy banks is impaired by the absence of financial statements on the bank exposure and also by lack of under accounting and reporting requirements.

The U.S Generally Accepted Accounting Principles (GAAP) relate to accounting standards including the conventions rules and procedures necessary to define accepted accounting procedures in a particular time. These include not only guidelines for general application but also detailed practices and procedures. The generally accepted principles are conventional being accepted by agreement rather than by formal concepts. The principles have been developed on the basis of experience, reason, custom, and usage and by practical necessity. The two broad categories of accounting are measurement and disclosure. While the former determine the timing and basis of items entering the accounting cycle in influencing the financial statements. The disclosure principles deal with factors that are not always numerical. These involve qualitative features that comprise the financial statements. They compliment measurement standards by explaining them and by giving other information on accounting policies, contingencies and uncertainties essential in the accounting process.

In advanced countries where markets are mature along with regulations, accounting standards give higher weightage to relevance to enhance the decision usefulness of financial statements. There has been a shift away from historical cost based accounting to fair value based accounting. Fair values enable the users to predict future cash flows, their amount timing and riskiness along with financial and operational transparency. In the era of globalized banking the need arises for harmonization in accounting and removing the obstacles to interventional comparability of financial statements. In India the Accounting Standards Board (ASB) was set up in 1977 by the Institute of Chartered Accountants of India (ICAI) to harmonize diverse accounting policies through the formulation of various accounting standards. So far it has formulated 16 accounting standards. They are:

1. Disclosure of accounting policies
2. Valuation of inventories
3. Cash flow statements
4. Contingencies and events accruing after the balance sheet date
5. Net profit or loss for the period
6. Depreciation accounting
7. Accounting for construction contracts
8. Accounting for Research and development
9. Revenue reorganization
10. Accounting for fixed assets
11. Accounting for the effects of changing in foreign exchange rates
12. Accounting for government grants
13. Accounting for investments
14. Accounting for amalgamation
15. Accounting for retirement benefits in the financial statements and borrowing cost.

The Financial Accounting Standards Board (FASB) has adopted predictive value approach in the USA; from 2001 it is also involved in the creation of high quality global accounting standards. In the US GAAP annual reporting has to make risk and return relationship more transparent provide share holders and depositors with overall professional management expertise and give management an opportunity to renovate the financial statements with its own insights. Multiple set up is a popular form for profit and loss account, income statement and statement of earnings. In this case cost of goods sold is deducted from sales revenue to show gross margin while either expenses will be subtracted to derive operative income. Non operating revenue expenses gains and losses are reported separately from operating items and income tax is deducted as the last item. Lending is considered, as originating fees is required over the life of the loan as an adjustment of its yield resulting in an adjustment of interest income. For the balance sheet the popular format is the report form showing a downward sequences of total assets and stockholders equities. Loans have to be stated at their outstanding principal amount net of unearned income, net of unmortized differed fees and costs with an allowance for credit loss. When there is uncertainty in the ultimate collection of principal or interest loan could be put under non-accrual status. In this case collections are applied as a reduction to principal outstanding. In the case of restructured loans concessions, reduction of the interest rate or deferral of interest or principal would be granted if the financial position of the borrower is weak.

In the case of investment trading securities are valued at fair value and unrealized gains or losses are included in earning. Non current assets are valued at historical cost and revaluation to current market value is not allowed. Non current liabilities are reported of the present value of future cash payments. The United States has been the first country to require a statement of cash flows on activity format in terms of operating. Investing and financing activities. Reconciliation of net income to cash flows from operating activities, wherein interest paid is reported, dividends paid are shown under financing activities while cash inflows from sales come under investing activity. Investing and financing activities not affecting cash are to be reported either in a supplementary form. Under rule 14a-3 of the Securities and Exchange Act of 1934, public companies must include description of business activities. Summary of selected financial data, selected quarterly financial data, segment information, market price of stock, list of directors, disagreement with accounting, personnel and discussion and analysis of financial condition and results of operation. The discussion and analysis has to focus on liquidity, capital resources and results of operations.

In the US controlling financial interest means ownership by one enterprise over 50 per cent of the outstanding voting shares of another enterprise. In India control means the ownership through subsidiaries of more than 50 per cent of the voting power of the enterprise or control of the composition of the governing body. The Reserve Bank has required the banks to prepare and disclose consolidated financial statements from April 2002 in addition to existing solo financial statements. Under international accounting standards the parent company consolidates financial statements unless it is wholly owned (as a subsidiary) and the parent obtains the approval of the owners of minority interest.

In the case of investment (US GAAP) securities can be 'held to maturity', at amortized cost, trading securities at fare value or available for sale at fare value. In India 'held maturity' securities are valued at acquisition cost while that or 'held for trading' are valued at market price. The book value of securities will change with revaluation. 'Available for sale' securities are valued scrip wise, with aggregation of depreciation and appreciation. Under the IAS, current investment are readily realizable, valued at market or at the lower of cost and market are intended to held for upto 1 year long term investment are valued at cost.

Under income taxes asset and liability approach is used in US GAAP in income tax accounting. In India the income statement approach of accounting considers differences between profit chargeable to tax and profit as per the profit and loss statement (accounting income). As permanent differences do not reverse subsequently no differed tax asset or liability is created. The IAS emphasizes the balance sheet approach and current tax becomes a liability. Impairment is measured for certain investment is debt and equity market. Impaired loans are measured based on the present value of expected future cash flows discounted at the loans affective interest rate. Changes are reflected in income and as adjustments to allowance for credit losses. In Indian GAAP recently RBI has made the banks to adopt the US GAAP to deal with NPAs. Under the international accounting impairment losses have to be recognized when the recoverable amount of asset is loss than its carrying amount. Discount rate has to be a pre tax rate.

Public enterprises have to report financial and descriptive information about their portable operating segments. In India segmentory reporting is mandatory for those enterprises where equity and debt securities are listed in a stock exchange and the enterprises which are in the process of issuing equity that will be listed on a recognized stock exchange in India. Disclosure is required in the case of total cost incurred during the period to acquire segment assets. Further disclosure in total amount of depreciation and amortization is also required under Indian GAAP. Under IAS segment reporting formats are business and geographic. Primary segment includes disclosures, assets and liabilities and cost to acquire property, plant, depreciation etc. Secondary segment disclosures are in revenue, carrying amount of segment assets, cost to acquire property and basis of intersegment pricing. Under US GAAP, material related party transactions are carried out on an armslength basis. Related parties include disclosure nature of relationship, description of transactions and amounts due from or to related parties. Under Indian GAAP, related party disclosures include party relationships and transactions between reporting enterprises and related parties. The latter includes disclosures such as description of relationships and elements and valueness of transactions under IAS where control exists related party relationships are disclosed irrespective of whether transactions have taken place.

Whatever may be the control system transgression by noted companies like Enron, Worldcom, etc which resulting in their collapse. Due to creative accounting profits had been overstated by 20 per cent , reducing the share holder equity to make good the liabilities of the partnership. The Enron failure highlights the failure of internal credit committee of the broad to police their auditors. The RBI appointed advisory group is international accounting and auditing there is a need for banks to adopt international accounting practices to attract more capital from abroad.

The banks require adequate capital and provisions of maintain a healthy financial system at the same time limiting the risk. Capital requirements in the past reflected rules of thumb or resulted from political negotiations. According to Basel committee on banking supervision (1999) capital and provisions control credit risk by creating a buffer against credit losses. The general provision in requirement could be recorded as Tier II capital against requirement while Tier I capital is considered as core capital including equity capital and published reserves from post tax from retained earnings. Tier II capital is supplementary including hybrid capital instruments, subordinated debt and provisions. The capital accord requires that at least 50 per cent of capital used to meet minimum levels as to be Tier I capital. While provisions alone can protect banks against ordinary levels of credit loss. Capital requirements protect them against unforeseen losses. If provisions reflect the expected value of credit losses, capital requirements protect against unexpected losses. Both provisioning and capital requirements may be specified from the same distribution of potential credit losses but they reflect different statistics of that distribution. According to the Basel committee, aggregate amount of specific and general provisions should be adequate to absorb estimated credit losses that are association with the loan portfolio. According to that committee most sophisticated banks view and capital as covering unexpected as opposed to expected losses. Provisions and capital requirements are supplemented by the interest that banks charge to compensate for the expected cost of default. Net interest is supposed to cover the losses expected at the moment of origination and the non-diversifiable portion of unexpected losses. Interest may compensate for expected losses and systematic risk partly duplicating the roles of provisions and capital. However, according to the Basel committee provisions will be adequate to protect against expected losses without interest margin. Net interest may be available as protection only if it is not first paid as a dividend to bank share holders. When shareholders expect normal return provisions will cover normal losses without the inclusion of net interest earnings when banks portfolio deteriorates, in order to increase provisions, the bank may reduce or ever suspend dividend payments.

If retained earnings are appropriated into a disclosed reserve, it will be Tier I capital otherwise the accumulated after tax surplus of retained profits may be included as Tier II capital. The profits may be observed not merely expected subjects to the limits on Tier II capital if not appropriated into a reserve. Many countries have adopted Basel 1988 capital accord not only to international active banks but also domestic banks. In some, requirements have been stricter than minimum of 8 per cent of asset at risk. Risk weights for different assets capture the different levels of risk in their returns. These weights may be complementing with a risk indicator based on the interest rate charged on each loan. Loans with higher interest rates have a higher capital requirement owing to higher levels of risk. Capital requirements include factors that depend on capital, assets, management liquidity, earnings and sensitivity rating assigned to the banks. This Basel capital requirement does not take into account how individual exposures are combined in the loan portfolio. One Rs. 100 crore loan, in a single company has the same capital requirement as 1000 loans of Rs. 1 lakh each to 100 different companies if these loans are in the same risk category. A diversified portfolio may reduce the total credit risk and requirements do not differ according to the level of correlation of asset return in a portfolio. The rules have reflected the actual risk of credit portfolios; otherwise capital allocation decisions may be distorted. The banks may use their own measures of credit risk to determine capital requirement. However, the correct shape of loss distribution has not been resolved and the short span of historical data does not validate the credit risk models properly. Further, operational risks have not been adequately studied. For normal asset current position has been 1 per cent , the percentage of provision being 5 per cent of potential risk, 25 per cent for substandard asset, 50 per cent for doubtful asset and 100 per cent for loss. Many countries adopt credit risk + model to quantify the credit risk which has been developed by Credit Swiss financial products, portfolio based credit risk models highlight the concentration of exposures in large borrowers and the correlation of changes in credit quality of separate borrowers. If the exposure is limited to a few large borrowers, their default can create larger than expected total assets. Further default may cause in branches resulting in a higher than expected default rate. In many cases actual provision requirements have been found closed to the employed resources.

Recent analysis shows that there has been an improvement of the status of commercial banks after a slowdown in the totality of financial sector assets and liabilities (EPW RF 2002). During the eighties the share of bank deposits in the annual increase in total household financial assets had declined from 45.8 per cent in 1980-81 to 32 per cent in 1990-91. By 2000-001 addition to gross held assets through bank deposits increased to 41.2 per cent owing to the weak performance of primary capital market including other funds term financing and investment institutions and non banking companies. Financial assets of banks, which constituted 73.8 per cent of total assets of the financial system in 1981, declined to 65.5 per cent in 1991 and 62.9 per cent in 1998. But the share increased to 66 per cent in 2000-01. Even the governments small saving collection showed a decline from 13.4 per cent in 1990-91 to 13.1 per cent in 2000-01. However banks are yet to deliver newer forms of credit including project finance and factory and till finance have not taken of.

The NPAs of banks and financial institutions are estimated to be more than Rs. 100,000 crore. An ordinance of regulates securitization and reconstruction of financial assets and enforcement of security interest is in the offering.. According to this asset reconstruction or securitization company will have to own funds of not less than Rs. 2 crore or not exceeding 15 per cent of total financial assets to be acquired. The acquisition can be through debentures or bonds and on acquisition the company can offer security receipts to qualified institutional buyers. The company may take over the business of the borrower or change the management; sale or base of the business reduce the payments of debts of the borrower and enforce the security by taking possession of secured assets. The company acts as an agent of a bank and act as receiver. The ordinance provides for enforcement of security interest without intervention of the court or tribunal. RBI may prescribe prudential norms in income recognition, accounting standards, and provisioning and capital adequacy to be followed by the securitization of reconstruction company besides prescribing the type of financial asset to be acquired along with aggregate value.

Once an account becomes NPA the bank can give notice to pay all liabilities within 60 days failing which it can take possession of secured assets of the borrower, take over management of such assets, manage the secured assets and realize the money due to any person who has enquired any of the secured asset from the borrower. If the dues are not fully recovered through the secured assets, the bank may file an application for recovery of balance amount. The borrower if agreed may appeal within 45 days from the date of such measures being taken. Default in filing changes relating to transaction of securitization or asset reconstruction or security interest creative or modification to the effect of satisfaction or a fine may be levied. No reference shall be made to the BIFR after commencement of the ordinance incase financial assets have been acquired. The degree of effectiveness of the ordinance depends upon rules and regulations to be formulated regarding detailed procedure of transactions, central legislation and RBIs guidelines. However permission of BIFR may be required in certain uses. The ordinance favours the creditors, by maintaining balance between the needs of borrowers and creditors. Asset management companies facilitate cleaning up of balance sheet of banks thus getting scale benefits.

Credit Disbursal

The member bank credit accounts declined from 6.2 crore in 1992-93 to 5.7 crore in 1995-96 and further to 5.2 crore in 1998-99 (CMIE 2000). The credit outstanding was Rs. 1625 billion in 1992-

93 increasing to Rs. 2547 billion in 199596 and Rs. 3824 billion in 1998-99, giving per account credit as Rs. 26200, Rs. 44600 and Rs. 73500 respectively in the three years. The proportion of agricultural credit has been declining from 13.6 per cent in 1992-93 to 11.3 per cent in 1995-96 and 10.7 per cent in 1998-99, the proportion of agricultural account deckling from 42 per cent during the first two periods to 38 per cent in the terminal year. The proportion industry accounts increased in the later period, the share of industry credit showing an increase from 48.6 to 49.2 per cent during the period. In agricultural credit the proportion of direct credit is very high even though that of indirect credit has been slowly on the increase. Industry textiles, food processing, chemical and basic metals share bulk of the credit. The proportion of transport credit share has shown a decline from 2.3 to 1.9 per cent during the period. There has been an increase in professional services, personal loans (including housing credit) and finance accounts while there has been a decline in trade and SSI accounts.

Of the total bank credit, the share of State bank group has been 30.83 per cent in 1992-93, declining to 29.15 per cent in 1995-96 and 28.12 per cent in 1998-99. The share of nationalized banks declined from 54.3 to 51.05 and to 49.19 per cent during the three periods. The share of foreign banks increased from 7.44 to 8.19 per cent while the increase has been from 2.82 to 2.95 per cent in the case of RRBs and from 4.61 per cent to 11.5 per cent in the case of private and other banks.

In the State bank group, the proportion of agricultural accounts declined from 43.2 per cent in 1992-93 to 39.1 per cent in 1998-99 while the share in credit declined from 14.2 to 11.9 per cent during the period. The share of industry accounts increased from 9.2 to 11.1 per cent while the credit share increased from 53. per cent to 53.9 per cent. There has been a decline in the artisans account from 3.7 to 3.1 per cent , the credit share showing an increase from 0.5 to 0.7 per cent. The SSI accounts showed an increase from 4.4 to 5.7 per cent while the credit share declined to 9.9 from 10.3 per cent. The average credit amount per agricultural account increased from Rs. 9800 to Rs. 24000 while the increase per industry account has been from Rs. 1.72 to Rs. 3.92 lakh.

In the case of nationalized banks the decline in agricultural account has been from 39.8 to 36.1 per cent and in the credit share from 13.6 to 10.8 per cent. The increase in the industry accounts has been from 8.2 to 9.0 per cent , the credit share showing a slight decline from 47.2 to 46.3 per cent. The artisans account showed an increase. 2.6 to 2.8 per cent in accounts and from 0.5 to 0.6 per cent in credit while the SSI accounts increased from 3.6 to 4.5 per cent , the credit share declined to 8.5 per cent (from 13.6 per cent). The per agricultural account credit increase has been from Rs. 10,000 to 24,000 while the increase in industry credit has been from Rs. 1.7 to Rs. 4.1 lakh.

In the case of foreign banks, agriculture, industry and SSI accounts have a very low share though in credit industry shared more than 60 per cent. The proportion of agricultural accounts in RRBs was 50.8 per cent in 1992-93 with an equal share in credit, but the account share declined to 41.1 per cent. In 1998-99 the credit share showing a slight decline to 49.1 per cent. The decline in industry accounts has been from 10.8 to 8.7 per cent , the credit share declining from 8.7 to 7.2 per cent. The artisans account shared a decline from 9.1 to 7.1 per cent , the credit share declining from 6.7 to 4.7 per cent. The SSI share has remained more or less constant at 1.5 per cent in number and 1.7 per cent in amount. The per agricultural account credit increased from Rs. 3530 to Rs. 10120 while the increase in per industry credit has been from Rs. 2850 to Rs. 8390.

In the case of private and other commercial banks agricultural accounts remarked more or less constant at 22.3 per cent , the credit share declining from 7.4 to 4.7 per cent. There was an increase in industry accounts (4.4 to 6.4 per cent), the credit share showing an increase (33.4 to 49.9 per cent). The artisans account remained the same at 1.1 per cent in number and 0.2 per cent in amount, while the SSI accounts showed an increase (2.1 to 3.1 per cent) its credit share showing a decline (11.6 to 9.1 per cent).

Private companies were the major borrowers from the commercial banks-38.6 per cent in 1992-93 increasing to 42.6 per cent in 1995-96 and to 48.1 per cent in 1998-99. The proportion of other enterprises in total credit showed an increase from 26.2 to 27.7 per cent declining to 22.4 per cent in the third period. The share of individuals declined from 16.8 to 9.1 per cent during the period, central government undertakings maintaining a constancy (around 11 per cent). While the share of state government increased from 0.5

to 1.4 per cent the share of state government undertakings declined from 2.3 to 1.8 per cent , that of quasi government bodies from 1.23 to 1.16 per cent and that of cooperative sector from 2.1 to 1.5 per cent during the period. Industry, finance and trade have been the major areas where bulk of the credit was borrowed by the aforesaid institutions.

Of the total credit the share of less than Rs. 25,000 was 19.8 per cent in 1992-93 declining to 14.2 per cent in 1995-96 and the 10 per cent 1988-99 while above Rs. 10 crore share increased from 16.4 to 20 and further to 29.1 per cent during the three periods. Between Rs. 25,000 to Rs. 5 lakh there has been an increased share while between Rs. 5 lakh to Rs. 6 crore there has been a declining share. Above Rs. 6 crore loans have increased their shares from 5.2 to 6.4 per cent.

The rate of interest charged on the credit ranged from less than 6 per cent (2.82 per cent in 1992-93 and 0.3 per cent in 1998-99) to over 20 per cent (26.1 and 4.9 per cent respectively). The average interest rate was more than 15 per cent during the first period, more than 17 per cent during the second period but during the third period, it was between 12-18 per cent.

Of the total bank credit, the proportion of rural population has been 18.7 per cent declining to 14.1 per cent during the period; a decline in semi urban population has been from 15.6 per cent to 14.3 per cent. The urban population too showed a decline from 20.7 to 18.5 per cent , indicating the bulk of bank credit going to the metropolitan population (45 to 53.1 per cent).

The per capita credit has been very high in Delhi (Rs. 15018) followed by Chandigarh (Rs. 12339), Maharashtra (Rs. 4524), Goa (Rs. 4177). In 1992-93, Bihar having the lowest per capita credit at Rs. 514. During 1998-99 the per capita credit increased to Rs. 49083 in Chandigarh, Rs. 30072 in Delhi, Rs. 11757 in Goa and 10192 in Maharashtra in Bihar it was Rs. 830, Nagaland showing the lowest amount at Rs. 778. In Karnataka it increased from Rs. 1984 to Rs. 3380 and further to Rs. 4869 during the three years.

Of the total deposits outstanding, Maharashtra's share is about 20 per cent , that of Delhi and U.P each 10 per cent , West Bengal 7.4 per cent , Tamil Nadu 6.6 per cent , Karnataka 5.5 per cent , Kerala 4.7 per cent and Orissa, 1.5 per cent. The per capita deposit has been over Rs. 60,000 in Chandigarh followed by Delhi and Goa (over Rs. 40,000) Maharashtra and Kerala (over Rs. 10,000) Tamil Nadu and Karnataka (over Rs. 7000) and others.

Deposits maturing in less than 90 days accounted for 13.1 per cent in 1992-93 but their share declined to 8.9 per cent in 1998-99, the share of 91 days to 5 years showing an increase. There has been a decline in the above 5 year's deposits (15.4 to 11.8 per cent).

Of the total bank assets the share of cash and bank balance has been 17 per cent in 1995-96 which declined to 15.4 per cent in 1999-2000. The share of advances, receivable and net fixed capital showed a decline while increased its share from 31.8 to 37.1 per cent. Of the total advances, the share of short term declined from 73.2 to 63.6 per cent while that of term loan increased from 26.8 to 36.4 per cent. The share of priority sector slightly declined from 28.2 to 28 per cent and the share of outside India advances declining from 8.7 to 6.8 per cent

Of the total liabilities the share of deposits increased from77.7 to 81.2 per cent during the period, that of borrowings declining from 7.7 to 4.7 per cent , that of other liabilities and provisions from 10.6 to 9.3 per cent , that of capital from 2.6 to 1.1 per cent while there has been an increase in the share of reserve fund and surplus from 1.5 to 3.8 per cent.

Financial cost accounted for bulk of the operating cost 60.6 per cent followed by personal cost (15.5 per cent) contingency (6.6 per cent), tax (4.0 per cent) and others. Profit before depreciation and tax was 3.8 per cent of operating income in 1995-96 increasing to 12.7 per cent in 1998-99 while profit after tax share increased from 1.76 to 7.25 per cent. Profit before depreciation and taxation as a percentage to total asset increased from 0.4 to 1.31 per cent while that of profit after tax showed as increase from 0.19 to 0.75 per cent.

The average cost of deposit increased from Rs. 6.89 to Rs. 7.11 during the period while the average return on advance declined from Rs. 12.43 to Rs. 10.65. The net interest spread has been 1.5 per cent declining to 1.44 per cent. The return on investment remained at around 11.3 per cent. The credit deposit ratio declined from 48.8 to 45.1 per cent. While the incremental credit deposit ratio declined from 83.0 to 53.4 per cent.

The growth of deposits has been around 12 per cent during 1995-96 increasing to 17.7 per cent per annum during 1999-2000. The growth rate in advances was around 21 per cent in both the years while there has been a decline in the borrowings rate from 71 to 21.3 per cent. The growth rate in total income (26 to 15.7 per cent) interest income (27.7 to 9.1 per cent) total cost (29 to 11.2 per cent), personnel cost (26.5 to 10.5 per cent), provisions (19.6 to 10.1 per cent) and interest expended (28-15 per cent) all shared a decline.

The proportion of profit after tax as a percentage of total assets increased from 0.57 to 0.79 in the State bank group and from 0.38 to 0.59 per cent in the nationalized banks while there has been a decline in the case of private banks (1.2 to 0.91) and foreign banks (1.5 to 1.2 per cent).

Bank Credit to GDP Ratio

The proportion of total credit to GDP was 18.6 per cent in 1980-81 increasing to 21.7 per cent in 1985-86, 22.4 per cent in 1990-91 and 23.6 per cent in 1999-2000. The proportion of agricultural credit to agricultural GDP has been very low at 7.8 per cent during 1980-81 increasing to 8.9 per cent in 1999-2000 indicating a rather poor performance. The proportion of industry credit to industry GDP increased from 37.3 to 43.1 per cent during the period. Tertiary credit as proportion to tertiary GDP increased from 17.7 to 21.2 per cent.

The proportion of credit to GDP has been very high in the northern region, 32.4 per cent in 1980-81 and 31.7 per cent in 1998-99. Delhi and Chandigarh have a very high ratio-88 per cent in 1998-99 whereas the ratio has been around 20 or less the Punjab, Haryana, Rajasthan and Himachal Pradesh. Only in Jammu and Kashmir the ratio is over 30 per cent. In the north eastern region the ratio has remained at 8.7 per cent during the period. The ratio has been higher in Assam and Tripura (less than 10 per cent) and lower in others. In the eastern region also, the ratio remained at around 16 per cent , West Bengal having a higher ratio (19.3 per cent). The ratio is 11 per cent in central region increasing to 12.9 per cent in the terminal year. Madhya Pradesh had an above average ratio (14.5 per cent). The ratio in the western region has been 29.4 per cent slightly increasing to 31.3 per cent. The ratio has been higher in Maharashtra (35.8 per cent) followed by Goa and Gujarat. The ratio has been 24.5 per cent in the southern region, Tamil Nadu leading with 33.5 per cent and followed by Karnataka (26.5 per cent), Kerala (20.8 per cent) and others.

Of the total outstanding bank credit, household sector accounts for over 99.5 per cent of accounts as on March 2000, the share remaining more or less same since March 1980. However its share in credit limit has been 35.9 per cent in 2000 showing a decline from 40.5 per cent in 1980. Its share in the amounts outstanding has been 37.1 per cent , down from 43.3 per cent. Private corporate sector's share in credit limit has increased from 35.8 to 47.9 per cent , its share in amount outstanding increasing from 32.9 to 45.9 per cent during the period. Public sectors share in credit limit has declined from 23.7 to 16.2 per cent , the decline recorded in the case of amount outstanding also to 17.0 per cent. During 1980-85, variation in credit limit in the household sector has been 167.6 per cent , declining to 161.5 per cent during 1985-1991 and 109.4 per cent during 1991-2000. Variations in outstanding has been 174.5 per cent during 1980-1985, 185.6 per cent during 1985-1991 and 104.8 per cent during 1991-2000. The credit limit variation in the private capital sector has been 63.9, 163.9 and 411.8 per cent respectively while in amount outstanding the variation has been 76.6, 222.4 and 360.2 per cent respectively. In the case of public sector the variation has been 85.4, 24.4 and 391.1 per cent in credit limit and 118.1, 24.6 and 392.5 per cent in amount outstanding during the three periods. For all the institutional categories the credit limit variation increased from 111.2 in the first period to 133.7 per cent during 1985-1991 and to 235.5 per cent in 2000. In amount outstanding the variation has been 129 per cent during the first period 158.6 per cent in the mid year and 217 per cent in 2000.

Residents own 57 per cent of total deposits in the banks followed by wages and salary earners (14.9 per cent), businessmen (12.8 per cent) farmers (10.7 per cent), giving a total of 66.7 per cent to individuals, 10.8 per cent to other institutions, 7.7 per cent to financial corporate sector, 7.1 per cent to government sector and 6.8 per cent for non financial corporate sector. When compared to 1982 the share of the institutions has substantially increased and in the case of individuals that of non-residents.

In total advances the share of 27 public sector banks has declined from 84.6 per cent in 1994-95 to 77.5 per cent in 2000-01. The share of SBI group has declined from 30 to 27.6 per cent and that of 19 nationalized banks from 54.5 to 49.9 per cent. The share of 31 private banks has increased from 7.3 to 13.8 per cent and that of foreign bank (42) from 8.1 to 8.7 per cent. As regards priority sector over 83 per cent advances is being met by PSBs the share of private banks being 10.9 per cent and that of foreign banks 6 per cent.

As regards to NPAs as percentage of total assets the ratio has declined from 7.03 per cent in 1997-98 to 5.32 per cent in 2000-01 in the case of gross NPAs and from 3.27 to 2.72 per cent in the case of net NPAs for the PSBs. The share of NPAs is slightly for the SBI group and higher for the nationalized banks. The share is 3.7 per cent gross and 2.26 net for the private banks and 3.02 gross and 0.79 per cent net for the foreign banks during 2000-01. Amongst the PSBs Indian bank, Allahabad bank, UBI, Dena Bank and UCO Bank have higher NPAs, so also the old private banks.

The proportion of operating expenses has been 2.99 per cent of total assets in 1995-96 declining to 2.72 per cent in 2000-01 in the case of PSBs. The decline has been higher in the SBI group (3.1 to 2.66) than in the nationalized banks (2.93 to 2.76 per cent). For the private banks the decline has been from 2.46 to 1.87 per cent while the foreign banks have registered an increase from 2.77 to 3.05 per cent. Some banks like Indian bank, Bank of Rajasthan, Grindlays bank etc have had increased operating expenses during the period.

The proportion of interest expended has been 6.12 per cent in 1995-96 declining to 5.99 per cent of total assets in 2000-01 in the case of PSBs the share being lower for the SBI group and higher for the nationalized banks and private and foreign banks. The proportions of interest income has shown a decline from 9.2 to 8.84 per cent of total assets in the PSBs the share being lower for SBI groups and higher for nationalized banks, private and foreign banks. Of the 52,000 bank branches existing in 2000-01 PSBs account for 89.5 per cent (SBI group 26.2 and nationalized banks 63.3 per cent). Private sector banks 10.1 per cent (old banks 8.6 and new banks 1.6 per cent) and foreign banks 0.4 per cent. When compared to 1994-95 the share of PSBs has shown a decline by 1.7 per cent.

The per branch staff in numbers has declined from 20.5 in 1994-95 to 17.2 in 2000-01 in the case of PSBs, 24.31 to 21.5 in the SBI group, 18.8 to 15.5 in the nationalized banks, 13.4 to 13.2 in the private banks, 13.4 to 12.8 in the old private banks, 19.8 to 15.1 in the new private banks and from 87.8 to 74.8 in the case of foreign banks.

The income of all banks in India has been Rs. 858.6 billion in 1997-98 and Rs. 1153.9 billion in 1999-2000. In this the share of State bank group has shown an increase from 29.0 to 29.5 per cent while the nationalized banks have shown a decline from 49.9 to 49.3 per cent. The share of PSBs remained more or less at 78.9 per cent , the old and new private banks slightly improving their share indicating a decline in the share of foreign banks (10.1 to 9.0 per cent).

Total expenditure by all the banks has increased from Rs. 793.6 billion to Rs. 1080.8 billion during the period showing a slight increase in the share of PSBs and new private banks and declined in the share of old private and foreign banks. Net profit has increased from Rs. 65 to Rs. 73.1 billion the share of PSBs declining from 77.4 to 70.0 per cent while the share of private and foreign banks increasing correspondingly. The operating profit increased from Rs. 146.4 to Rs. 184.2 billion, the share PSBs remaining at around 70 per cent in both years and that of private banks showing a slight increase, while the foreign banks have a reduced share (17.4 to 14.6).

Total interest income has increased from Rs. 737.5 to Rs. 995.1 billion, the share of PSBs slightly down (80.1 to 79.9 per cent), in the old private banks no change (7.5 per cent), new private banks increasing the share (3.2 to 4.5 per cent) while foreign banks registered a decline (9.2 to 8.2 per cent). The proportion of income has declined from 10.8 to 10.4 per cent of total assets for all the banks. In the SBI group the income share has declined from 10.7 to 10.1 per cent while it has remained constant in the nationalized banks (10.3), indicating a slight decline in the PSBs (10.4 to 10.2 per cent). The decline has been 11.7 to 11.3 per cent in the old private and to 92 per cent in the new private banks and from 13.4 to 12.5 per cent in the foreign banks. Still the foreign banks have a higher share of assets in the form of income. There has been a decline in expenditure from 10 to 9.7 per cent the decline significant only in the new private and foreign banks. The proportion of net profit to total assets has declined from 0.82 to 0.66 per cent for all the banks. The decline has been from 0.77 to 0.57 per cent in the 27 PSBs, from 1.06 to 0.8 per cent in the SBI group and from 0.62 to 0.44 per cent in the nationalized banks. The old private banks have slightly improved their ratio from 0.81 to 0.84 per cent while in the new private banks the decline has been from 1.55 to 0.97 per cent. Foreign banks had greatly improved their performance from 0.97 to 1.17 per cent during the period. The share of interest has slightly declined from 9.3 to 9.0 per cent for all the banks the decline substantial in the new private banks (7.5 per cent). There has been a slight decline in the operating expenses (2.6 to 2.5 per cent) the decline notable in the new private banks while the foreign banks had an increase (3 to 3.2 per cent. In the case of wage bill there has been a slight decline from 1.8 1.7 per cent for all the banks, the share in the new private banks being the lowest (0.3 per cent) and also in the foreign banks (1.0 per cent of assets). While there is no change in the provisions (10 per cent) for all the banks private banks had a slightly declining share (1.2 to 10 per cent in old private and 1.3 to 1.2 per cent in the new private banks), the foreign banks declining their high share from 2.9 to 2.1 per cent. The proportion of interest spread has declined from 2.95 to 2.72 per cent for all the banks indicating an improved efficiency. The decline has been from 2.91 to 2.7 per cent in the PSBs, 3.14 to 2.76 per cent in the SBI group, 2.78 to 2.67 per cent in the nationalized banks, 2.57 to 2.33 per cent in the old private sector banks, 2.32 to 1.87 per cent in the new private sector banks and from 3.93 to 3.85 per cent in the case of foreign banks.

5
RURAL BANKING
A Case study

Introduction

In the new Dakshina Kannada district 38 financial institutions including scheduled commercial banks-PSBs, private banks, RRBs, cooperative banks and others have been participating in the annual credit plan. Some 33 banks were participating in the erstwhile Dakshina Kannada district. As on March 1989 there were 454 bank branches which have been reduced to 333 (plus around 145 in Udupi district) as on March 2002. The per branch deposits has increased from Rs. 2 crore in 1989 to Rs. 14 crore in 2002. The per branch advance increased from Rs. 1.36 to Rs. 6.4 crore during the period, indicating a higher rate of deposit growth. The credit deposit ratio, which was 68 per cent , is only 46 per cent now. During 1995-96 it was only 41 per cent. Of the total priority sector advances, agricultures show the total priority sector advances, agriculture share was 23 per cent in 1997-98, 35 per cent in 1998-99, 30 per cent in 1999-2000, 26 per cent in 2000-01 and 30 per cent in 2001-02 indicating an average allocation of 30 per cent over the years. Allocation on SSIs has remained at around 32 per cent , slightly higher that of agriculture. There has been a slight increase in the case of retail trade small business, self-employment, housing finance to weaker sections and on small road and water transport (between 4-10 per cent in each).

In 1998-99 for a total of 322 bank branches per branches advance has been Rs. 4.1 crore and the priority sector allocation has been

43.3 per cent. The share of agriculture in PSA has been 38.4 per cent followed by SSI (33.1 per cent) small road and water transport (8.9 per cent) retail trade (7.3 per cent) and others. The credit deposit ratio has been 45 per cent and total direct agriculture advance 15 per cent of all advances. In 1999-2000 the per branch advance increased to 4.9 crore with a share of 46.4 per cent for the priority sector. Agricultural advances declined to 30 per cent of PSA and direct agriculture advances to 12 per cent of total advances. The share of SSI increased to 36.9 per cent of PSA followed by retail trade (10.2 per cent) small road and water transport (7.7 per cent), weaker section housing (7.6 per cent) and others. The credit deposit ratio remained at 4.5 per cent. During 2000-01 the per branch advance increased to Rs. 5.5 crore with PSA share increasing to 49.6 per cent. The share of agriculture declined to 25.7 per cent of PSA. The share of direct agriculture in total advances declined in 11 per cent. The share of SSI too declined to 31 per cent of PSA followed by small road and water transport (10.6 per cent) retail trade (9.8 per cent) weaker section also (8.6 per cent) and others. The credit deposit ratio increased to 46 per cent which remained at that level during 2001-02 also. In that year the per branch advance increased to RS. 6.5 crore, PSA share declining to 43.8 per cent. The share of agriculture slightly increased to 29.9 per cent of PSA but that of direct agriculture declined to 8 per cent of total advances. The share of SSI remained at 32 per cent followed by small road and water transport (9.5 per cent) retail trade (8.6 per cent) weaker section also (6.6 per cent) and others.

Total deposits in the district have been 11.14 lakh, the share of Mangalore being 63.9 per cent followed by Bantwal (12.6 per cent), Puttur (12.4 per cent) Belthangady (7.6 per cent) and Sullia (3.5 per cent). The per account deposit has been Rs. 18593 for the district, Mangalore having a higher average (Rs. 22748) and others having around Rs. 11,000 each. The total number of advance accounts has been 1.23 lakh the share of Mangalore being 55.6 per cent followed by Bantwal (14.0 per cent), Puttur (13.8 per cent), Belthangady (8.7 per cent) and Sullia (7.9 per cent). The per account advances has been Rs. 91421, higher in Mangalore (Rs. 124981) followed by Belthangady (Rs. 54348), Sullia (Rs. 51884), Puttur (Rs. 50963) and Bantwal (Rs. 43547). The following table presents a summary of bank branches taken for analysis.

Bank	*Bantwal*	*Puttur*	*Sullia*	*Belthangady*	*Mangalore*
SBI	04	01	—	02	30
SBM	—	02	01	—	09
Canara	08	04	06	01	51
Syndicate	14	13	11	18	53
Vijaya	19	17	12	12	51
Corporation	03	03	02	02	33
Karnataka	12	03	01	03	20
NGrB	02	04	04	06	03
PCARD	02	02	02	02	01
SCDCCB	04	10	06	07	13
Others	—	—	02	—	60
Total	68	59	47	53	324

Priority Sector Advances

Total priority sector advances amounted to 64,220 which is 52.3 per cent. Mangalore accounted for 36.1 per cent of PSAs in the district followed by Bantwal (21.7 per cent) Puttur (180 per cent), Sullia (12.4 per cent) and Belthangady (11.8 per cent). The proportion of PSA to total advances has been 81 per cent in Bantwal and Sullia 71 per cent in Belthangady, 68 per cent in Puttur and 34 per cent in Mangalore. The per account PSA advance has been Rs. 82401 in the district, being higher in Mangalore (Rs. 146261) followed by Puttur (Rs. 54827), Belthangady (Rs. 50581), Bantwal (Rs. 45336) and Sullia (Rs. 31707). The overage priority sector advance has been higher in Bantwal, Mangalore and Puttur when compared to total advance. The share of agricultural advance has been 50 per cent for the district the proportion being 54 per cent in Bantwal 56 per cent in Belthangady, 66 per cent in Sullia, 98 per cent in Puttur and only 16 per cent in Mangalore. The average agricultural advance has been Rs. 40532, higher in Mangalore. About 89 per cent of agricultural advances have been direct with a lower average (Rs. 25240 for the district) while indirect advances were with over Rs. 1.3 lakh each. In Bantwal the share of SSI has been 3.7 per cent of PSA the average loan amount being Rs. 2.55 lakh. The proportion of non-farm sector is 8.7 per cent with an average advance of Rs. 40,000. The share of other priority sector has been 33.3 per cent with an average of Rs. 36,676. The share of weaker sections has been 64.4 per cent with an average advance of Rs. 15,102. The SC/ST beneficiaries accounted for 10.8 per cent with an average of Rs. 12789. The proportion of IRDP accounts has been 10.3 per cent with an advance of Rs. 6878. Those who have benefited under direct rate of interest accounted for 1.3 per cent per unit advance being Rs. 5665. The number of small and marginal farmers accounts have been 32 per cent with an average of Rs. 19544. The proportion of artisans benefited has been 6.2 per cent with an average of Rs. 11529. Some 3.7 per cent of other weaker sections have Rs. 15663. About 17.5 per cent of the PSA belong to women (Rs. 19572) and some 25 per cent to minorities (Rs. 22407). Those benefited under PMRY account for 3.2 per cent with an average advance of Rs. 33596 and other government programmes 3.5 per cent (Rs. 8988). The proportion of PSA has been 84.5 per cent and that of weaker sections 18.1 per cent. The credit deposit ratio has been 47.62 per cent.

In Belthangady, the proportion of SSI accounts has been only 2.4 per cent with an average of Rs. 1.2 lakh. The proportion of non far sector has been 7.9 per cent (Rs. 55150) OPS 33.4 per cent (Rs. 63450) weaker sections 96 per cent (Rs. 15102). SC/STs accounting for 10.6 per cent with Rs. 12789). The proportion of DRI advance has been only 0.4 per cent with Rs. 2782 while IRDP accounted for 25 per cent with RS. 4460 as advance. The small and marginal farmers accounted for 45.5 per cent (Rs. 19610), artisans 5.5 per cent 9Rs 36200), other weaker sections 9.1 per cent (Rs. 15,200), women 18.5 per cent (Rs. 34314) and minorities 21.8 per cent. The share of PMRY has been 3.4 per cent with an investment of Rs. 49441. The proportion of other government programmes has been 9.5 per cent with an advance of Rs. 27000. The share eof PSA in total advance has been 65.5 per cent with improved CD ratio (62.7 per cent).

In the new Udupi district there are 19 banks with 223 branches. The per branch deposit has been Rs. 49 crore and advance Rs. 4.1 crore as on March 2002. The total credit plan of the district has been Rs. 414 crore, the percentage of disbursal being 130. The share of PSA has been 52.5 per cent. The share of agriculture and allied activities has been only 7 per cent , SSI and tiny sector 19 per cent , tertiary and other priority sector 21.3 per cent the rest being non priority sector. In the total credit plan however the allocation has been primary 13 per cent , secondary 30 per cent , tertiary 29 per cent and non-priority 29 per cent. The share of syndicate bank with 61 branches has been 36 per cent followed by Corporation bank (17 per cent), Canara Bank (13 per cent), SCDCC bank (12 per cent), Vijaya Bank 5.3 per cent), Karnataka bank (4 per cent) and others. In the district total Udupi followed by Kundapur and Karkal in agriculture, Karkal followed by Udupi and Kundapur in SSI and Udupi followed by Kundapur and Karkal in tertiary sector had a higher share. In the total PSA of the district share of Udupi has been 43 per cent , that of Karkal 35 per cent and that of Kundapur 22 per cent. In the total plan outlay Udupi's share has been 50 per cent followed by Karkal (27 per cent) and Kundapur (23 per cent). The share of PSA in Syndicate Bank has been 70 per cent , in Vijaya Bank 59 per cent , in Corporation Bank 70 per cent , in Canara Bank 92 per cent , in Karnataka bank 65 per cent , in SCDCC Bank 62 per cent and in Netravati Grameena Bank 73 per cent.

In Mangalore the total number of deposit accounts have been over 7 lakh being 64 per cent of the district total, the per account deposit amount being Rs. 22748. The total number of advance accounts has been 6.8 lakh (55.6 per cent at district total) the average advance being Rs. 1.25 lakh. The share of PSA accounts has been 3.4 per cent with a higher advance amount of Rs. 1.46 lakh. The proportion of agricultural advance has been 15.7 per cent with a lower amount of Rs. 0.82 lakh. The bulk of the agricultural advance has been direct (Rs. 0.46 lakh), the smaller share of indirect advance being over Rs. 40 lakh. The share of SSI has been 19.4 per cent with over Rs. 3 lakh. The share of non-farm sector has been 4.8 per cent with Rs. 0.8 lakh. The share of tertiary sector has been 60 per cent with over rupees one lakh. The proportion of weaker sections benefited has been 21 per cent with an average advance of Rs. 17,583 and that of SC/STs 2.9 per cent with Rs. 15700. The proportion of IRDP advances has been 3.6 per cent with an average advance of Rs. 9752. The proportion of DRI accounts has been 0.2 per cent with an average of Rs. 3896. Some 10 per cent of the accounts are by small and marginal farmers the average amount being Rs. 14054. About 1.2 per cent of the artisan accounts are Rs. 65633. The share of other weaker sections has been 2.5 per cent with an average advance of Rs. 27894. Women beneficiaries account 32.3 per cent with an average loan of Rs. 50563. The share of minorities has been 31.7 per cent with an average loan amount of Rs. 96491. The proportion of PMRY accounts has been 3.9 per cent , the average loan amount being Rs. 56824 and other government programmes 2.3 per cent with a loan amount of Rs. 22642. The share of Agriculture to total advance has been 3.5 per cent , weaker sections 1 per cent , PSA accounting 40 per cent of total advances. The credit deposit ratio has been 52.7 per cent.

In Puttur, the total number of deposits has been 1.4 lakh being 12.4 per cent of the district total. The per account deposit rate has been low at Rs. 11390. In advances the share has been 13.8 per cent with an average loan of Rs. 50963. The share of PSA has been 68 per cent with an average loan amount of Rs. 54827. Agriculture accounts for over 98 per cent of PSA (in that bulk direct) the average advance being Rs. 34209 (Rs. 11742 for direct and Rs. 10 lakh for indirect). The SSI share is only 2.7 per cent with an average of Rs. 1.7 lakh. The share of NFS has been 3.1 per cent with an average loan of Rs. 65367. The share of tertiary (OPS) has been 20.2 per cent with a loan amount of Rs. 72381. In all, about 45 per cent of the accounts belong to weaker sections and 5.2 per cent SC/STs with a loan amount of Rs. 27846 for the former and Rs. 98679 for the other. The proportion of IRDP accounts has been 6.3 per cent with a loan amount of Rs. 8921. The DRI advances shared 0.4 per cent with an average of Rs. 24010. The small and marginal farmers advances accounted for 26.8 per cent with a loan amount of Rs. 36125 and artisans 1.2 per cent with Rs. 22536. Women accounts shared 11 per cent with Rs. 33080 and minorities 13.4 per cent with Rs. 28018. PMRY share has been 1.6 per cent (Rs. 72571) and that of other government programmes 1.3 per cent (Rs. 24603). The PSA share has been 73.5 per cent and agriculture in total advances shared 45.1 per cent. The credit deposit ratio has been 54.8 per cent.

In Sullia, total number of deposit accounts has been 38600, just 3.5 per cent of the district total. The per account deposit has been Rs. 11418 as against the district average of RS. 18593. The share of advance accounts has been 7.9 per cent with an average loan of Rs. 51884 to the districts Rs. 91421. In PSA the share has been higher at 12.4 per cent but the loan amount has been only Rs. 31707 to the district's Rs. 8240 per cent. The share of PSA in total advances has been 82# as against the district average of 52 per cent.

Shares of Other Sectors

Agriculture's share in PSA has been 66.3 per cent the average loan being Rs. 31464 to the district's Rs. 40532. The proportion of direct agriculture has been only 32 per cent of PSA (with Rs. 31963) and that of indirect advance 34.4 per cent (Rs. 31000). The district direct agriculture loan has been Rs. 252240 and that of indirect agriculture over Rs. 1.5 lakh. The share of SSI has been only 1.5 per cent with an average loan amount of Rs. 5190 as against Rs. 2.97 lakh for the district. The share of NFS has been 1.9 per cent with Rs. 54200 to the district's average of Rs. 58509. So the share of tertiary sector has been 30.3 per cent with Rs. 29922 to the district average of Rs. 82183.

The proportion of weaker sections' advance has been around 60 per cent and that of SC/STs 6.5 per cent in both cases the loan amount being around Rs. 20000 much higher than the district average. The proportion of IRDP accounts has been higher at 9.7 per cent with an average loan amount of Rs. 9871 while the average in DRI (0.3 per cent) the amount has been Rs. 2696. The proportion of small and marginal farmers has been 31 per cent with an average of Rs. 23229 much similar to the district total of Rs. 22599. The share of artisans has been 1.9 per cent with an average of Rs. 5046, to the district average of Rs. 25369. 10.2 per cent of PSA are other weaker section accounts where the average loan amount has been Rs. 24749, slightly higher than the district average. The share of women accounts has been 10.6 per cent with an average of Rs. 35542 slightly higher than the district average of Rs. 40647. The share of minorities has been 7.3 per cent , the loan amount being about 67 per cent of the district average of Rs. 63878. The PMRY share is only 1.8 per cent with Rs. 42158 lower than the district average and the other government programmes 1.5 per cent with Rs. 30881. The PSA share in total advances has been 49.9 per cent as against 47.1 per cent in the district and that of direct agriculture 32.9 per cent as against 11.6 per cent for the district. The credit deposit ratio has been quite high in Sullia at 114.2 per cent as against the district average of 54.2 per cent.

In Bantwal for the 24 bank branches per branch IRDP accounts have been around 60 with an average branch outstanding as Rs. 4.1 lakh. The average number of PMRY accounts has been 18.3 with branch outstanding as Rs. 6.1 lakh. The per branch other government programme accounts have been 20.5 with an outstanding of Rs. 1.8 lakh. The total number of these three accounts has been Rs. 2369. The per branch accounts being around 99, per branch outstanding being around Rs. 12 lakh. The per account outstanding has been Rs. 12257 the amount being higher in PMRY.

In Belthangady, for the 16 branches per branch IRDP accounts have been 117.6 with per branch outstanding of Rs. 5.2 lakh. The per branch PMRY has been 16.4 and outstanding Rs. 8.1 lakh for other government programmes per branch accounts have been 44.7, outstanding being Rs. 12 lakh. For the three programmes combined total number of accounts have been 2859, the per branch accounts being 1787, the per branch outstanding Rs. 25.4 lakh and per account outstanding Rs. 14235 higher in PMRY. For the 87 Mangalore branches the per branch IRDP accounts have been 9.5 with an outstanding of Rs. 0,9 lakh. The per branch PMRY accounts have been 10.3 with an outstanding of Rs. 5.9 lakh. The average for other programmes is 6 with an outstanding of Rs. 1.37 lakh. The combined accounts amount to Rs. 2253, the average per branch being 26 and outstanding being Rs. 8.2 lakh. The per account outstanding has been 31538, the average being Rs. 56824 in PMRY Rs. 22642 in other programmes and Rs. 9752 in IRDP.

In the 17 Puttur branches per branch IRDP average has been 43 accounts Rs. 3.8 lakh outstanding. The per branch PMRY accounts have been 10.7 with an outstanding of RS. 7.8 lakh. In other programmes the average has been 8.6 accounts and Rs. 2.1 lakh outstanding. For the 1058 accounts under the three programmes per branch, average number has been 62.2 and advances outstanding Rs. 13.7 lakh and per account outstanding Rs. 22034.

In Sullia the average for 13 branches has been 59.5 IRDP, 10.7 PMRY and 9.1 other programmes. The total being 79.3, the per branch outstanding has Rs. 5.9 lakh in IRDP, Rs. 4.5 lakh in PMRY Rs. 2.8 lakh in other programmes and Rs. 13.2 lakh for all. For the total of 1031 accounts the per account outstanding has been Rs. 16634.

In The district during 1999-2000 for 24 banks per bank IRDP accounts have been 235.5, the amount outstanding being Rs. 16.9 lakh. In PMRY per bank accounts have been 80, the outstanding amount being Rs. 40.8 lakh. In other programmes the average has been 83.2, the outstanding being Rs. 17.9 lakh. In all under these three programmes total number of accounts have been 9570 per bank average being 399 with an outstanding of Rs. 75.5 lakh. The per account outstanding has been Rs. 18940 in the district, being Rs. 50948 in PMRY, Rs. 21462 in other programmes and Rs. 7170 in IRDP.

Talukwise Analysis

During 1999-2000, of the total advances in the respective taluks the share of priority sector accounts has been 52.3 per cent for the district higher in Sullia (81.6 per cent) followed by Bantwal (81.2 per cent) Belthangady (70.4 per cent) and Puttur (68 per cent), Mangalore having the lowest share (34 per cent). The share of PSA in total amount of advance has been 47 per cent in the district, higher in Bantwal, Puttur and Belthangady, average in Sullia and lower in Mangalore. In both number and amount Bantwal tops the list followed by Puttur and Belthangady.

The share of agriculture and allied activities accounts is 26.2 per cent in the district the share in Mangalore being very low at 5.3 per cent. The share in amount has been 116 per cent for the district, ranging from 45 per cent in Puttur to 3.5 per cent in Mangalore. Puttur tops the list in having a larger number and amount share for agriculture. Proportion of direct agricultural accounts has been 23.3 per cent in the district ranging from 5.3 per cent in Mangalore to 66.5 per cent in Puttur. However in amount the share range has been from 2 to 25 per cent. This is because in the case of indirect agriculture advance the share especially in Puttur, Sullia and Bantwal has been very high.

The share of SSI accounts has been 4.6 per cent , Mangalore having a higher share at 6.6 per cent followed by Bantwal (3 per cent). In the other three taluks the share was less than 2 per cent. However in amount the share has been very high at 14.8 per cent. Mangalore and Bantwal having above this average, Sullia having the lowest share (1.2 per cent).

In the case of non-farm sector the share of accounts has been 2.8 per cent and that of amount 1.8 per cent. The number share has been higher in Bantwal (7 per cent) followed by Belthangady (5.6 per cent) and others; in amount also this trend is visible. The share of other priority sector (tertiary) is higher second only to agriculture. Its share in number has been 21 per cent and in amount 18.9 per cent. Bantwal, Sullia and Belthangady have a higher number share, while Belthangady, Bantwal and Puttur have a higher amount share. Puttur has a lower number share while in amount it is Sullia.

Of the above PSA beneficiaries the share of weaker sections is 25.3 per cent for the district (very low in Mangalore at 7 per cent) and the amount share being 5.1 per cent Mangalore having only 1 per cent share. The proportion of SC, ST beneficiaries has been 3.3 per cent but their share in advance has been only 0.5 per cent. The number share in Mangalore has been the lowest at 1 per cent and in amount only 0.13 per cent. Bantwal followed by Sullia and Belthangady has a higher share.

In respect of IRDP, Belthangady has the largest share of accounts (17.5 per cent) followed by Bantwal (8.4 per cent), Sullia (7.9 per cent) and Puttur (4.3 per cent), Mangalore having the lowest share (1.2 per cent). The share of amount for the district as a whole is only 0.4 per cent as against the number share of 4.6 per cent. Sullia had the highest share of 1.5 per cent followed by Belthangady (1.44 per cent) and Bantwal (1.32 per cent), Puttur had a share of 0.75 per cent , Mangalore having the lowest share at 0.09 per cent only. The proportion of DRI accounts and amounts has been very insignificant.

Of the total advance accounts the proportion of small and marginal farmers has been 12.8 per cent in the district with only 3.2 per cent share in the quantum of advance. Belthangady has the highest share of small and marginal farmers at 32 per cent , followed by Bantwal (over 26 per cent), Sullia (over 25. per cent), Puttur (over 18 per cent). The share was only 3.4 per cent in Mangalore, the taluk having the lowest amount share at 0.4 per cent. The per account quantum of assistance has been higher in Puttur where the amount share has been about 13 per cent followed by Bantwal and Sullia where the amount share has been over 11 per cent. In Belthangady though the amount share has been 11.6 per cent , the per account amount has been lower when compared to the above three taluks. The proportion of artisan accounts has been 1.5 per cent with an amount share of 0.4 per cent , Bantwal and Belthangady performing well under both the accounts. The proportion of other weaker section accounts has been 2.3 per cent. Sullia and Belthangady having higher portions and the amount share has been 0.6 per cent , Sullia, Belthangady and Bantwal having higher shares. The proportion of women accounts has been very high in Bantwal and Belthangady moderate in Mangalore and lower in Sullia and Puttur, the amount share has been higher in Belthangady, Bantwal and Sullia, lower in Puttur and Mangalore. The proportion of minority accounts has been around 12 per cent with a quantum share of 8.3 per cent , Bantwal and Belthangady having higher proportion in number of accounts and Belthangady, Bantwal and Mangalore having higher share in quantum. The proportion of PMRY accounts has been d1.6 per cent with account 1 per cent quantum share, Bantwal and Belthangady having higher shares in both the accounts. The proportion of other government programme has been 1.6 per cent with a quantum share of 0.4 per cent Belthangady and Bantwal having higher share in the accounts and Belthangady, Sullia and Bantwal having higher shares in both the kinds.

Service Area Approach

Under service area for the year 1998-99 total priority sector advance accounted for 60 per cent in number of accounts (Bantwal, Belthangady and Sullia having over 70 per cent) and 56 per cent in total advance amount (Belthangady, Sullia and Bantwal having over (75 per cent). The share of agricultural accounts has been 31 per cent in number of accounts and 18 per cent in amount. The share of SSI and other priority sector being 7 and 21 per cent respectively in accounts and 20 and 18 per cent in amount. Sullia, Bantwal and Belthangady in agriculture, Mangalore, Puttur in SSI, Belthangady and Bantwal in OPS have a higher share. The service area IRDP accounts have been in large in Belthangady and Sullia and Belthangady in amount. Under both IRDP and PMRY the share in amount has been the same (1.2 per cent), Belthangady and Bantwal having a higher share. The share of other sectors including NPS has been 30.8 per cent in the district in accounts (Mangalore and Puttur having over 50 per cent) and 42 per cent in amount (Puttur and Mangalore having over 50 per cent). In the next quarter the proportion in accounts slightly declines to 50.6 per cent and the amount increasing to 43.5 per cent , Puttur and Mangalore having very high shares.

In the case of banks the share of Syndicate and Vijaya bank in total advances is over 19 per cent each followed by agriculture and rural development/SCDCC bank (14.4 per cent), Canara bank (10.8 per cent) Corporation bank (8.1 per cent) Karnataka bank (6.2 per cent), State Bank of India (3.1 per cent) and Netravati Grameena

Bank (2.8 per cent). In amount disbursed Syndicate bank has the highest share at 22.4 per cent followed by Canara bank (17.9 per cent), ARD/SCDCC bank (12.1 per cent), Corporation Bank (8.5 per cent), SBI (5.4 per cent) and NGB (1.0 per cent). The total priority sector advance has been over 90 per cent in ARD/SCDCC bank, over 75 per cent in NGB, above 65 per cent in Vijaya Bank, Over 5.8 per cent in both SBI and Canara Bank, above 4.6 per cent in Syndicate Bank, 41 per cent in Karnataka Bank and 34 per cent in Corporation bank. NGB and ARD/SCDCC have a higher share of agricultural advances (93 per cent) in NGB) and 55 per cent in the latter. Except Vijaya Bank, the 31 per cent , whereas the district average is only 10.7 per cent , Canara, Corporation and Karnataka bank. In SSI, SBI, Canara and to some extent NGB have advanced in a greater measure to SSIs followed by Karnataka bank while Corporation and Vijaya Banks have very low share. GR and ARD/SCDCC bank followed by Corporation bank has had a higher share. Under IRDP advances the share in NGB followed by Vijaya Bank. Under PMRY, only Vijaya a Bank with a share of over 4 per cent was prominent. Corporation Bank and Karnataka Bank have in Belthangady and Puttur show statistical performance. Mangalore and Puttur have a low share in priority sector (less than 50 per cent) while the share is between 70-80 per cent in Sullia, Belthangady and Bantwal. In these three taluks agricultural advances are prominent whereas the SSI is prominent in Puttur and Bantwal. In OPS its Mangalore, Belthangady and Bantwal. Belthangady and Bantwal in IRDP and also in PMRY both have a higher share when compared to others. Puttur and Mangalore show higher share for NPA.

Syndicate Bank followed by Vijaya Bank ARD/SCDCC bank, Canara bank and Corporation bank. The share of priority sector advances in very high in ARD/SCDCC bank and NGB. ARD/SCDCC bank in SSI and besides that SBI topped in OPS share. NGB and Vijaya bank in IRDP and Vijaya Bank and SBI in PMRY have higher ratios. During that year the priority sector share has been over 88 per cent in ARD/SCDCC bank followed by NGB (77.5 per cent). Vijaya bank followed by Canara bank, SBI and Syndicate bank has over 50 per cent share while it is only around 35 per cent in Corporation and Karnataka bank.

The advances have been classified according to quantum of demand. The total priority sector demand has been 42.3 per cent of the total demand of Rs. 626.4 crore in the district. Of the total credit demand the share of Mangalore has been 79.3 per cent followed by Sullia 6.3 per cent , Puttur 6.2 per cent , Bantwal 4.3 per cent and Beltghangady 3.9 per cent. The share of priority sector advance has been 31 per cent in Mangalore 81.7 per cent in Puttur, 84.7 per cent in Belthangady, 90 per cent in Sullia and 84.2 per cent in Bantwal. The share of crop cultivation demand has been 11.1 per cent for the district, that of minor irrigation 0.8 per cent , land development 0.6 per cent , farm mechanization 0.5 per cent , plantation and horticulture crops 0.3 per cent , dairying 0.9 per cent , other animal husbandry 0.2 per cent , fisheries 0.3 per cent , agriculture labour development 2.1 per cent , SSI 16.1 per cent , other priority sector (trade) 8.7 per cent , IRDP 0.3 per cent and PMRY 0.5 per cent.

The proportion of recovery has been 96 per cent in crop cultivation, 73 per cent in minor irrigation, 76 per cent in land development, 92 per cent in farm mechanization, 82 per cent in plantation and horticulture, 96 per cent in Dairying, 48 per cent in other animal husbandry, 47 per cent in fisheries, 95 per cent in agriculture labour development, 77 per cent in NFS, 90 per cent in SSI, 76 per cent in OPS, 64 per cent in IRDP, 54 per cent in PMRY and 63 per cent in other programmes the recovery rate for NPS being 87.5 per cent and for PS and NPS combined 87.9 per cent.

In Bantwal the proportion of crop cultivation demand has been 40.3 per cent (95 per cent recovery), minor irrigation 0.3 per cent (63 per cent recovery), farm mechanization 0.1 per cent (84 per cent recovery), and animal husbandry having a very low share 0.1 per cent (with recovery rate of about 4.6 per cent). ALD 0.1 per cent (87 per cent recovery) NFS 0.2 per cent (84 per cent recovery) SSI 0.6 per cent (recovery 54 per cent OPS 2.2 per cent (80 per cent recovery), NPS 1.6 per cent (recovery 92 per cent) and IRDP and PMRY about 0.1 per cent in each with a recovery rate of 70 per cent in the former and 75 per cent in the latter. The combined recovery rate for all advances has been 85.2 per cent.

In Belthangady, the share of crop cultivation has been 20.1 per cent (87 per cent recovery), minor irrigation 4.6 per cent (71 per cent recovery) land development 3.5 per cent (81 per cent recovery), farm mechanization 6.3 per cent (98 per cent recovery), plantation and horticulture 0.8 per cent (6.6 per cent recovery). Dairy highest in whole district at 19.8 per cent (recovery 98 per cent), other animal husbandry and fisheries 0.3 per cent (90 per cent recovery), ALD 3.4 per cent (81 per cent recovery NFS 4.9 per cent (87 per cent recovery), SSI 2.2 per cent (88 per cent recovery) OPS 18.7 per cent (87 per cent recovery), NPS 5.2 per cent (88 per cent recovery), IRDP 1.7 per cent (66 per cent recovery) and PMRY 1.3 per cent (75 per cent recovery. The overall recovery rate in the taluk has been 89 per cent , giving an overdue of 11 per cent.

In Mangalore, the share of crop cultivation has been only 0.6 per cent (85 per cent recovery) that of minor irrigation being 0.1 per cent (76 per cent recovery), land development 0.1 per cent (72 per cent recovery), farm mechanization 0.05 per cent (83 per cent recovery, plantation and horticulture 0.2 per cent (88 per cent recovery), Animal husbandry 0.2 per cent (48 per cent recovery), fisheries 0.3 per cent (44 per cent recovery ALD 2.2 per cent (97 per cent recovery), NFS 0.4 per cent (74 per cent recovery), SSI 19.7 per cent (91 per cent recovery), OPS 7 per cent (73 per cent recovery), IRDP 0.1 per cent (59 per cent recovery), PMRY 0.4 per cent (49 per cent recovery) and NPS 69 per cent (87.5 per cent recovery). The overall recovery rate for the taluk has been 87.2 per cent , the proportion of overdues being 12.8 per cent.

In Puttur, the proportion of crop cultivation demand has been very high at 55.2 per cent (98 per cent recovery), that of minor irrigation being 3.3 per cent (76 per cent recovery), farm mechanization 1 per cent , (82 per cent recovery), plantation and horticulture 0.5 per cent , (69 per cent recovery), dairy 0.4 per cent (82 per cent recovery), other animal husbandry and fisheries 0.7 per cent (70 per cent recovery), ALD 1.5 per cent (79 per cent recovery), NFS 1.1 per cent (63 per cent recovery), SSI 1.9 per cent (only 38 per cent recovery), OPS 15 per cent (84 per cent recovery), IRDP 1 per cent (68 per cent recovery), PMRY 0.8 per cent (5.4 per cent recovery) and NPS 18.3 per cent (87 per cent recovery). The overall recovery for the taluk has been 90.8 per cent.

In Sullia too, the proportion of crop cultivation advances is very high at 74.2 per cent (98 per cent recovery) followed by NPS 9.6 per cent (85 per cent recovery), OPS 7.1 per cent (83 per cent recovery), minor irrigation, 2.8 per cent (80 per cent recovery), land development 2.1 per cent (80 per cent recovery), ALD and farm mechanization each 1.2 per cent (83 per cent recovery in the former and 91 per cent in the latter), IRDP 1 per cent (62 per cent recovery), PMRY 0.8 per cent (60 per cent recovery), Diary and SSI 0.4 per cent (70 per cent recovery in the former and 42 per cent in the latter), and plantation and horticulture 0.3 per cent (83 per cent recovery). The overall recovery rate is the taluk has been 94.6 per cent.

Groupwise Advances

An attempt has been made to classify the advances into different groups according to various activities. In the district in three banks advances to crop cultivation, plantation and horticulture crop exceed Rs. 10 crore the average per bank being Rs. 20.7 crore. The recovery rate has been 97 per cent. There are two accounts in the range of Rs. 2-5 crore, the average per bank being Rs. 3.9 crore. The percentage of recovery has been 86. One bank has the advance between RS. 1-2 crore the average being Rs. 1.1 crore with 88 per cent recovery. In four banks the advance has been less than 1 crore the average being 13.6 lakh with 71 per cent recovery.

In the case of minor irrigation and banks have an average 1.2 crore with recovery rate of 75.6 per cent and two banks Rs. 70.7 lakh with 70 per cent recovery. As regards land development and farm mechanization two banks have an average of Rs. 1.4 crore with 84.5 per cent recovery and 8 banks Rs. 12.5 lakh with only 20 per cent recovery. In all animal husbandry and fisheries activities 1 bank has an average advance of Rs. 4.9 crore (98 per cent recovery), another bank Rs. 1.6 crore (44.4 per cent recovery) and 16 banks have an average of Rs. 2.9 lakh with recovery rate of 21 per cent. In about 2 banks there have been no accounts under this group.

In the NFS and allied sectors like agriculture labour, and storage and marketing yard are five banks no accounts have been reported. On bank has ever Rs. 10 crore advance, the average being Rs. 11 crore with recovery of 95.7 per cent. One bank has an average of Rs. 2.2 crore with a recovery of 73.8 per cent. Another bank has an average of Rs. 1.2 crore with 87 per cent recovery. 12 banks have an average of Rs. 8.2 lakh with 26.1 recovery. In the case of SSI one bank has Rs. 98 crore with recovery of 91.7 per cent one bank has an average of Rs. 1.7 crore with 54 per cent recovery and three banks Rs. 47.6 lakh with 56 per cent recovery. One bank has an average of RS. 35.2 crore with 73.2 per cent recovery in OPS, two banks having an average of Rs. 5.9 crore with 82 per cent recovery and another two Rs. 3.7 crore with 85.3 per cent recovery.

In the case of NPS, one bank has an average of 34.3 crore with 87.3 per cent recovery, another bank Rs. 7.1 crore with 87 per cent recovery and three banks Rs. 3.9 crore with 88.3 per cent recovery. In the case of IRDP only 5 banks have advanced averaging Rs. 37.3 lakh with a recovery of 65 per cent. In the case of PMRY and other government programmes one bank has advanced Rs. 1.95 crore with a recovery rate of 48.8 crores and 9 banks Rs. 4.9 lakh with a lower recovery of 14.5 per cent.

In Bantwal in 15 bank branches, the average demand has been Rs. 75.9 lakh with recovery of 80.5 per cent. In one branch the average demand has been Rs. 5.7 lakh with recovery of 73.5 per cent. In two branches the average has been Rs. 3.2 lakh with 72.4 per cent recovery. Notice in three branches the average has been Rs. 0.53 lakh with 29 per cent recovery and in 9 Rs. 4000 with 20 per cent recovery. 8 branches have not advanced under these activities. In minor irrigation two branches have an average demand of Rs. 14.6 lakh with 70.6 per cent recovery, 6 branches Rs. 6.2 lakh with 58.4 per cent recovery and four branches Rs. 3.3 lakh with 52.4 per cent recovery. In your branches the average demand has been Rs. 1.5 lakh with 73 per cent recovery in 2 branches 0.93 lakh with 100 per cent recovery and in Rs. 0.23 lakh with 87.5 per cent recovery. In one branch no advance has been reported.

Five branches have an average demand of Rs. 21.5 lakh with 72 per cent recovery in the case of land development and farm mechanization. Two branches have an average of Rs. 7.5 lakh with 67.7 per cent recovery, 6 branches having an average of Rs. 1.2 lakh with 27 per cent recovery. The average demand has been Rs. 1.55 lakh in five branches with a recovery rate of 35.5 per cent , in the average being 0.65 lakh with 36 per cent recovery and in 7 Rs. 6,530 with 23.7 per cent recovery.

In the all combined animal husbandry 7 branches have an average demand of Rs. 1.37 lakh with 12 per cent recovery while 6 branches have 0.47 lakh with 20 per cent recovery and 20 branches have Rs. 3280 with 10 per cent recovery. In the case of NFS including forestry, Agricultural labour development and storage and market yard in one branch the average demand has been Rs. 30.6 lakh with 93 per cent recovery. In four branches the average was Rs. 5.3 lakh with only 41 per cent recovery. In seven branches the average has been 2.8 lakh with only 25 per cent recovery. In 3 branches the average has been 1 lakh with 57.5 per cent recovery. In five branches the average has been 0.6 lakh with 35.5 per cent recovery. The average has Rs. 4460 in 10 branches with a recovery of 12.4 per cent. In about four branches each there were no accounts under these activities. In the case of SSI there were no accounts in fifteen branches. The average demand has been 52 lakh in three branches (46.1 per cent recovery), Rs. 5 lakh in one branch (96.8 per cent) recovery, and Rs. 4.9 lakh in one chance (48.7 per cent) recovery). Rs. 1.8 lakh in one branch (54.9 per cent recovery) and 0.9 lakh in two branches (88.3 per cent recovery).

The number of branches that did not have OPS accounts has been 2 while in 19 branches the average demand has been Rs. 31 lakh (75 per cent recovery) while in two branches the average has been Rs. 4.3 lakh with 79.8 per cent recovery. In 6 branches there was no NPS accounts, the average demand in branches being Rs. 40.6 lakh (90 per cent recovery). The average has been Rs. 9 lakh in five branches (91 per cent recovery) and Rs. 4.2 lakh in 3 branches (75.7 per cent recovery).

There were no IRDP accounts in 10 branches and in five the average has been Rs. 3.4 lakh (70.3 per cent recovery), in 3 Rs. 1.7 lakh (82 per cent recovery), in two Rs. 0.7 lakh (37 per cent recovery) and in three Rs. 0.2 lakh with 37 per cent recovery. In PMRY and other programmes 11 branches did not have any accounts. The average has been Rs. 6.3 lakh in one branch (62 per cent recovery), Rs. 2.8 lakh in 8 branches (16 per cent recovery), Rs. 1.6 lakh in five branches (34.4 per cent recovery) Rs. 0.8 lakh in four cases (31.7 per cent recovery) and Rs. 1 lakh in 6 branches with 27 per cent recovery. In all the above there were no accounts in 39 per cent of the branches in one or more activity. The percentage has been 16 per cent for less than 0.5 lakh, 7.6 per cent in Rs. 1-2 lakh, 7.3 per cent in Rs. 0.5-1 lakh and 5.4 per cent in Rs. 5-1 lakh.

In Mangalore, the number of branches above 70 per cent of bank branches has no accounts in one or other of the activities. In crop cultivation, land development, animal husbandry and NFS the non-accounts have been higher. The number of branches having average demand of Rs. 14.6 lakh has been 12 and the recovery rate has been 14.3 per cent only. In four branches the average has been Rs. 8.6 lakh (47.3 per cent recovery) in four branches 2.5 lakh (35.7 per cent recovery), in eight branches 1.4 lakh (18.2 per cent recovery), in four

0.8 lakh (36.5 per cent recovery) and in 21 Rs. 1400 with recovery rate of only 4.2 per cent. In minor irrigation likewise the number of branches having nil accounts have been in higher. The average demand has been Rs. 15 lakh in two branches (77.3 per cent recovery), Rs. 3.4 lakh in five branches (73.7 per cent recovery), Rs. 1.1 lakh in one branch (68 per cent recovery), Rs. 0.6 lakh in three branches (69 per cent recovery) and Rs. 0.2 lakh in 15 branches (67 per cent recovery).

In land development and farm mechanization only 34 branches had accounts. The average was Rs. 17.5 lakh in one branch (89 per cent recovery) Rs. 6.8 lakh in 5 branches (30 per cent recovery), Rs. 2.3 lakh in five branches (29 per cent recovery), Rs. 1.1 lakh in four branches (30 per cent recovery), Rs. 0.7 lakh in 8 branches with 20 per cent recovery and lakh in 8 branches with 20 per cent recovery and Rs. 3130 in 11 branches with 15 per cent recovery.

In all animal husbandry more than 70 per cent of the branches did not have any accounts in one or other branches. The average advance has been RS. 16 lakh with only 10.5 per cent recovery in 7 branches, Rs. 7 lakh with 47.6 per cent recovery in 3 branches, Rs. 2.7 lakh with 11 per cent recovery in 17 branches, Rs. 1.2 lakh with 36 per cent recovery in 6 branches, Rs. 0.5 lakh with 96 per cent recovery in five branches and Rs. 0.12 lakh with only 4 per cent recovery in 48 branches. In the NFS sector again many branches did not have any accounts. The average demand has been Rs. 19.8 lakh with 15 per cent recovery in 10 branches, Rs. 6.9 lakh with 22 per cent recovery in 8 branches, Rs. 2.6 lakh with 13 per cent recovery in 16 branches, Rs. 1.7 lakh with 37 per cent recovery in 7 branches, Rs. 0.5 lakh with d21 per cent recovery in 11 branches and Rs. 3020 with 11 per cent recovery in 21 branches.

In the case of SSI 31 branches did not have any accounts while in 65 branches the average demand has been Rs. 0.6 lakh with 56 per cent recovery. The average has been Rs. 1.1 lakh with 65 per cent recovery in four branches, Rs. 2696 lakh with 97 per cent recovery in three branches and Rs. 2.4 lakh with 77 per cent recovery in one branch. There has been no OPS accounts in the taluk and in 17 branches NPS accounts were also absent. In this activity 66 branches had an average of Rs. 0.52 lakh with 74 per cent recovery while the average has been RS. 1.4 lakh with 85 per cent recovery in 11 branches, RS. 3.5 lakh with 90 per cent recovery in 5 branches, Rs.

6985 lakh with 92 per cent recovery in 4 branches and Rs. 9.3 lakh with 85 per cent recovery in one branch.

In 79 branches out of over 105 there were no IRDP accounts. In one branch the average demand has been RS. 11.9 lakh with 48 per cent recovery, Rs. 6.5 lakh with 57 per cent recovery in one branch Rs. 2.8 lakh with 54 per cent recovery in three branches, RS. 1.4 lakh with 73 per cent recovery in 10 branches, Rs. 0.6 lakh with 91 per cent recovery in one branch and Rs. 0.2 lakh with 37 per cent recovery in 9 branches. In respect of PMRY and other government programmes the average demand has been RS. 0.1 lakh with 43 per cent recovery in 35 branches, Rs. 0.7 lakh with 63 per cent recovery in 19 branches, Rs. 1.1 lakh with 55 per cent recovery in 23 branches, Rs. 2.1 lakh with 34 per cent recovery in 29 branches, Rs. 6.5 lakh with 36 per cent recovery in 11 branches and Rs. 10.9 lakh with 45 per cent recovery in one branch.

In Belthangady, in respect of crop cultivation, plantation and horticulture, six branches did not have any accounts. The average has been 42.5 lakh with 80 per cent recovery in 6 branches, Rs. 5.7 lakh with 53 per cent recovery in 3 branches, Rs. 2.3 lakh with 25 per cent recovery in 5 branches Rs. 1.8 lakh with 38 per cent recovery in 3 branches and Rs. 0.1 lakh with 80 per cent recovery in 4 branches. In minor irrigation one branch did not have any accounts. The average in one branch RS. 18.7 lakh with 77 per cent recovery; the average in 11 branches has been Rs. 7.5 lakh with 70 per cent recovery, in 3 branches Rs. 3.3 lakh with 49 per cent recovery, in one branch Rs. 1.4 lakh with 76 per cent recovery and in another branch Rs. 0.4 lakh with 75 per cent recovery.

In land development and farm mechanization 13 branches have no accounts. In three branches the average has been Rs. 54 lakh with 61 per cent recovery, in 5 Rs. 5.5 lakh with 31 per cent recovery, in 3 Rs. 2.6 lakh with 63 per cent recovery, in 5, Rs. 1.2 lakh with 24 per cent recovery in 2 Rs. 0.7 lakh with 60 per cent recovery and in 5 Rs. 8900 with 35 per cent recovery. In all animal husbandry groups more than 12 branches did not have any accounts in one or other activity. 12 branches have an average demand of Rs. 4880 with 21 per cent recovery while in 6 branches the average is Rs. 1.5 lakh with 67 per cent recovery, in 4 Rs. 2.2 lakh with 60 per cent recovery, in 3, Rs. 0.6 lakh with 65 per cent recovery and in one Rs. 47.1 lakh with 100 per cent recovery. In NFS more than 13 branches have no accounts in one or other groups. The average in 5 branches has been Rs. 16.1 lakh with 33 per cent recovery, in two Rs. 65 lakh with 81 per cent recovery, in one Rs. 2.7 lakh with 26 per cent recovery, in two Rs. 1.3 lakh with 76 per cent recovery, in 4 Rs. 0.6 lakh with recovery of 65 per cent , and in 10, Rs. 3500 with recovery of only 10 per cent. In SSI, 8 branches have no accounts. The average demand has been Rs. 13.2 lakh in two branches, Rs. 7.1 lakh in three branches, Rs. 2.9 lakh in one branch, Rs. 1.7 lakh in two branches and Rs. 0.2 lakh in two branches. The rate of recovery ranged from 32 per cent in the last group to 94 per cent in the first group. In OPS one branch did not have any demand while 16 branches have a demand of Rs. 287 lakh each and in one Rs. 3.7 lakh, the recovery rate being 85 per cent in the former and 93 per cent in the latter. Four branches have no accounts in NPS while 10 branches have an average demand of Rs. 35.5 lakh, two branches Rs. 7.2 lakh and another two Rs. 4.1 lakh, the recovery rate range being 92 to 98 per cent. In IRDP, two branches have no accounts, in one the average has been Rs. 5.1 lakh, in 8, Rs. 3.7 lakh, in three Rs. 1.3 lakh, in two, Rs. 0.8 lakh and in another4 two Rs. 0.37 lakh, the recovery rate ranging from 58 to 75 per cent. More than ten branches have no accounts in PMRY and other government programmes. The average demand has been Rs. 3.9 lakh in ten branches (17 per cent recosvery) while it is Rs. 4.5 lakh in four branches (72 per cent recovery), Rs. 0.95 lakh in one branch (26 per cent recovery) and Rs. 7000 in one branch with 86 per cent recovery. In this taluk also the number of non-accounts is greater than the in-accounts.

More than 5 branches in Puttur do not have any accounts in crop cultivation, plantation and horticulture. In 11 branches the average demand has been Rs. 188.6 lakh with 92 per cent recovery, Rs. 8.5 lakh in two branches with 72 per cent recovery, Rs. 2.7 lakh in three branches with 49 per cent recovery, Rs. 0.7 lakh in one branch with 51 per cent recovery and Rs. 8380 in 6 branches with d28 per cent recovery. In minor irrigation one branch does not have any account, the average demand in 6 branches being 14.6 lakh with 71 per cent recovery, Rs. 8 lakh in three branches with 90 per cent recovery, Rs. 3.2 lakh in four branches with 81 per cent recovery, Rs. 1.5 lakh in two branches with 81 per cent recovery and Rs. 0.2 lakh in two branches with 100 per cent recovery.

The number of branches that have no accounts in land development and farm mechanization. In 8 branches the average demand has been 5.6 lakh with 21 per cent recovery, Rs. 2.1 lakh in seven branches with 24 per cent recovery, Rs. 1.3 lakh in four branches with 39 per cent recovery, Rs. 0.86 lakh in two branches with 7.6 per cent recovery and Rs. 6570 in six branches with 32 per cent recovery. In the animal husbandry sector eleven branches do not have any accounts. The average demand is one branch has been Rs. 19.3 lakh, in two Rs. 3.6 lakh in four Rs. 1.7 lakh in 8 Rs. 0.66 lakh and in eleven Rs. 5130 with the recovery rate ranging from 21 to 90 per cent. In the NFS sectors, seven branches do not have any accounts while three branches have an average of Rs. 14.5 lakh, another three Rs. 5.4 lakh. In four branches the average has been Rs. 2.5, lakh Rs. 1.2 lakh and Rs. 7130 and in seven branches Rs. 0.54 lakh. The range of recovery being between 35 to 64 per cent.

In SSI, eight branches have no accounts, the average in one branch being Rs. 50.8 lakh in another branch, Rs. 5.1 lakh, in three branches Rs. 3 lakh, in another three Rs. 1.8 lakh, in one Rs. 0.96 lakh and in another 0.2 lakh, the recovery rate range being from 31 to 100 per cent. One branch does not have any OPS accounts, while 13 have an average of 42.3 lakh, three Rs. 7.9 lakh, and one Rs. 4.4 lakh with recovery rate of 49 to 91 per cent. In NPS three branches have no accounts while in nine the average has been Rs. 76.2 lakh, in one Rs. 9.4 lakh in two Rs. 3.1 lakh and in three branches Rs. 1.6 lakh, the range of recovery being 51-92 per cent. There are no IRDP accounts in two branches while the average is s 6.3 lakh in two branches, RS. 3.4 lakh in four branches, Rs. 1.5 lakh in 6 branch, Rs. 0.7 lakh in three branches and Rs. 0.4 lakh in one branch, the recovery rate ranging from 60-100 per cent. In some seven branches there were no PMRY and other programmes accounts the average in one branch being Rs. 9.6 lakh, in five Rs. 2.1 lakh in another five Rs. 1.6 lakh in six Rs. 0.7 lakh and in four Rs. 0.4 lakh the recovery ranging from 20 to 75 per cent.

In Sullia, the average demand has been Rs. 264 lakh in eleven branches in crop cultivation, plantation and horticulture, while the average has been Rs. 5.4 lakh in three branches, Rs. 2.5 lakh in one branch, Rs. 1.1 lakh in three branches, Rs. 0.56 lakh in one branch and Rs. 5000 in another branch. In minor irrigation the average has been Rs. 15.1 lakh in five branches, Rs. 7.4 lakh in two branches, Rs. 4.1 lakh in three branches, Rs. 1.5 lakh in four branches and in land development and farm mechanization six branches having Rs. 14.4 lakh, three Rs. 5.1 lakh, five Rs. 2.3 lakh, one Rs. 1.3 lakh, another one Rs. 0.7 lakh and two Rs. 0.2 lakh. The number of branches having no accounts in animal husbandry have been over ten; the average in one branch being Rs. 17 lakh, in three Rs. 3.8 lakh, in two Rs. 1.2 lakh and in t 12, Rs. 2830. In NFS too six branches have no accounts while the average has been Rs. 12.5 lakh in two branches, Rs. 2.1 lakh in nine branches, Rs. 1.1 lakh in two branches, Rs. 0.7 lakh in three branches and Rs. 6110 in six branches. In SSI, seven branches have no accounts while the average has been Rs. 8.6 lakh in one branch, Rs. 3.5 lakh in two branches, Rs. 0.5 lakh in one branch and Rs. 0.3 lakh in three branches. In OPS 12 branches have an average demand of Rs. 24.3 lakh, one branch Rs. 6.3 lakh, another Rs. 4.5 lakh and yet another RS. 0.6 lakh. In NPS the average has been Rs. 50.4 lakh in seven branches, Rs. 6.8 lakh in two branches, Rs. 3.8 lakh in three branches and Rs. 0.76 lakh in one branch. While the number of branches having no IRDP accounts has been two, one branch has an average of Rs. 12.1 lakh another Rs. 6 lakh, five Rs. 3.9 lakh, two Rs. 1.9 lakh, another two Rs. 0.7 lakh and one 0.47 lakh. In PMRY and other programmes. Six to seven branches have no accounts in either of them. The average demand has been Rs. 10.9 lakh in one branch Rs. 6.8 lakh in another branch, Rs. 2.9 lakh in three, Rs. 1.7 lakh in four, Rs. 0.7 lakh in five and Rs. 0.17 lakh in two. In all these cases the recovery has ranged from 27 per cent to 100 per cent.

For the district as a whole, the recovery rate has been Rs. 89.3 per cent and per taluk the average demand has been Rs. 1.3 crore. In Bantwal for 23 bank branches the total demand has been Rs. 1.17 crore, 15 branches having less than Rs. 1 crore average (Rs. 51 lakh with 79 per cent recovery) while four branches have between Rs. 1 to 2 crore (average Rs. 1.5 crore with 85 per cent recovery), one branch between Rs. 2 to 5 crore (Rs. 2.5 crore with 83 per cent recovery) and one in the Rs. 5 to 10 crore group (Rs. 5.6 crore with 97.7 per cent recovery). For the 18 branches in Belthangady the average demand has been Rs. 1.37 crore, 12 branches having less than Rs. 1 crore average (Rs. 61 lakh with 79 per cent recovery), 6 branches in the Rs. 1 to 2 crore group (Rs. 1.4 crore with 85 per cent recovery) and 1 branch in the 5 to 10 crore group (Rs. 9.6 crore with 98 per cent recovery). In Mangalore of the 104 branches 61 have less than Rs. 1 crore average (Rs. 48.7 lakh with 68 per cent recovery) 20 in the Rs. 1 to 2 crore (Rs. 1.4 crore with 73 per cent recovery), 15 in the Rs. 2 to 5 crore group (Rs. 3 crore with 64 per cent recovery) two branches in

Rs. 5-10 crore group (Rs. 8 crore with 85 per cent recovery) and 6 branches in the above Rs. 10 crore group (Rs. 63 crore with 93 per cent recovery). The average demand for the taluk has been Rs. 4.77 crore per branch.

For the 18 branches in Puttur, the average demand per branch has been Rs. 2.14 crore. In the less than Rs. 1 crore group there are eight branches with an average demand of Rs. 61.6 lakh with a recovery rate of 77 per cent , 4 branches in the Rs. 1 to 2 crore group with an average of Rs. 1.36 crore at a recovery rate of 83 per cent , five branches in the Rs. 2-5 crore group with an average demand of Rs. 3.6 crore and a recovery rate of 92 per cent and one branch in the over Rs. 10 crore group with an average of Rs. 10 crore with 99 per cent recovery. In Sullia the per branch demand has been Rs. 2.82 crore for 14 branches. There are seven branches in less than Rs. 1 crore group with an average of Rs. 61 lakh and 82 per cent recovery, four branches in Rs. 1-2 crore group with an average of Rs. 1.4 crore and 79 per cent recovery, one branch in Rs. 2.5 crore group with an average of RS. 3.2 crore and full recovery, one branch in the Rs. 5-1 crore group with an average demand of Rs. 7 crore with 98 per cent recovery and 1 branch in the over Rs. 10 crore group with an average of Rs. 19.3 crore with 99 per cent recovery.

During 2001-02, the total number of deposit accounts in the district is 16.35 lakh and the total amount of deposits is Rs. 3548.7 crore, the per account deposit being Rs. 21705. The share of Mangalore in total accounts has been 66.4 per cent followed by Bantwal and Puttur (11.1 per cent each), Belthangady (6.5 per cent) and Sullia (4.8 per cent). In the total deposit amount the share of Mangalore taluk has been even higher at 80.3 per cent followed by Puttur (6.7 per cent) Bantwal (6.3 per cent), Belthangady (4.2 per cent) and Sullia (2.5 per cent). The average amount per deposit account has been high at Rs. 26000 in Mangalore and lowest in Sullia at around Rs. 11000. The total number of advance accounts has been around two lakh in the district, Mangalore showing the largest share (53.5 per cent), followed by Puttur, Belthangady, Bantwal and Sullia in order of importance. In advance amount of Rs. 1905 crore in the district, Mangalore's share is highest at 76.2 per cent followed by Puttur (10.1 per cent), Sullia (4.8 per cent), Bantwal (4.6 per cent) and Belthangady (4.3 per cent). The credit deposit ratio for the district has been 53.6 per cent , the ratio being 102.5 in Sullia, 80.7 in Puttur, 55.9 in Belthangady, 50.9 in Mangalore and only 39.3 per cent in

Bantwal. The average advance per account has been Rs. 97470 for the district, the amount in Mangalore being Rs. 1.39 lakh, Rs. 0.61 lakh in Puttur, Rs. 0.56 lakh in Sullia, Rs. 0.41 lakh in Bantwal and 40.37 lakh in Belthangady.

The percentage of PSA to total advances has been 55.3 per cent in number and 46.4 per cent in amount for the district as a whole. In the district total the share of Bantwal have been 13.3 per cent in number and 7.2 per cent in amount, that of Belthangady's, 16.4 per cent in number and 7.8 per cent in amount. That of Mangalore 38.7 per cent in number and 63.5 per cent in amounts, that of Puttur 21.3 per cent in number and 12.9 per cent in amount. And that of Sullia 10.3 per cent in number and 8.5 per cent in amount. In the respective taluk, PSA's share has been 67.8, in number and 72.9 per cent in amount where compared to total advances in Bantwal. In Belthangady the number share has been 79.7 per cent and amount share 83.8 to total advances in taluk. In Mangalore the number share is only 40 per cent and the amount share is 38 per cent. In Puttur the number share has been 73.7 per cent and 68.7 per cent in Sullia while the amount share has been 59.2 and 82.7 per cent respectively. This indicates that Belthangady and Sullia more than 80 per cent of total advances are in the priority sector while the percentage in Bantwal has been over 70 per cent, around 60 per cent in Puttur and less than 40 per cent in Mangalore.

Share of Advances

Of the total PSA agricultural advances account for 54.3 per cent in number and 33.6 per cent in amount while the share of SSI has been 2.5 per cent in number and 21 per cent in amount, that of NFS 7.5 per cent in numbers and 7.6 per cent in amount and OPS 35.8 per cent in number 37.7 per cent in amount. The director agricultural advances accounted for 85.6 per cent in number 88.7 per cent in amount.

In Belthangady, the share of agricultural advances to PSA has been 41.3 per cent in number and 41.8 per cent in amount, that of SSI 29 per cent in number and 4.5 per cent in amount, that of NFS 6.8 per cent in number and 10.2 per cent in amount. And that of OPS 50 per cent in number 43.5 per cent in amount. The proportion of direct agricultural advance has been 87.4 per cent in number only 64.1 per cent in amount. In Mangalore, the share of agricultural advances has been 16.2 per cent in number and 8.5 per cent in amount to PSA while that of SSIs 11.8 per cent in number and 42.4 per cent in amount, NFS 4.8 in number and 3 per cent in amount and that of OPS 67.2 per cent in number and 46.1 per cent in amount. The share of direct agricultural advances has been 98.7 per cent in number and 83.5 per cent in amount.

In Puttur, agricultural advances account for 63.8 per cent in number of 58.6 per cent in amount while SSI show has been 1.6 per cent in number and 6.7 per cent in amount, that of NFS 3.5 per cent in number and 4.2 per cent in amount and that of Ops 31.1 per cent in number and 3(.5 per cent in amount. The share of direct agricultural advance has been 88.7 per cent in number and 56.3 per cent in amount. In Sullia, agricultural advances have a higher share in PSA 78 per cent in number and 76 per cent in amount while SSIs share has been 1.4 per cent in number and 4.2 per cent in amount that of NFS being around 1 per cent in both number and amount and that of OPS around 19 per cent in both. The percentage of direct agricultural advances has been 90 in number and only 48 per cent in amount indicating a huge advance indirect agriculture.

For the direct as whole share of agriculture has been 41.9 per cent in number followed by OPS (47.6 per cent), SSI (5.6 per cent) and NFS (4.8 per cent), in amount share of agriculture has been 25 per cent that of SSI 30 per cent , NFS 3.9 per cent and that of OPS 41 per cent. The share of direct agriculture has been 90 per cent in number and 64 per cent in amount.

In the total agricultural advance in the district, the share of Puttur is 30 per cent followed by Sullia (25.9 per cent), Mangalore (21.4 per cent), Belthangady (13.1 per cent) and Bantwal (9.7 per cent). However, in direct agricultural advance the share of Mangalore has been the highest (28. per cent) followed by Puttur (26.3 per cent), Sullia (19.3 per cent), Bantwal (13.3 per cent) and Belthangady (13.1 per cent) of the district total. In the number of advances Puttur has the largest share, Belthangady having the lowest (15.7 per cent).

In the number of SSI accounts, Mangalore has more than 80 per cent share and in amount share it has about 90 per cent indicating the over concentration of SSIs in the taluk. The number share in Bantwal is 5.8 per cent , the amount share being 5.1 per cent. In Puttur, the amount share is 2.9 per cent for the number share of 5.9 per cent. In Belthangady the respective shares have been 1.2 and 5.5 per cent and in Sullia 1.2 and 2.7 per cent respectively.

In NFS, Mangalore has the highest number and amount share (38.6 and 49.4 per cent) respectively) followed by Belthangady (23.1 and 20.6 per cent) respectively, Bantwal (20.5 and 14.2 per cent respectively), Puttur (15.5 and 13.9 per cent respectively) and Sullia (2.2 and 1.8 per cent respectively). In OPS advance again Mangalore has the highest share in both number (55 per cent) and in amount (71 per cent) followed by Puttur, Belthangady, Bantwal and Sullia in the order of importance.

In the different taluks, the proportion of PS demand to total advances outstanding is 57.7 per cent in the district, Sullia having the highest share (74.7 per cent) followed by Puttur (61.4 per cent), Mangalore (57.4 per cent), Belthangady (52.2 per cent) and Bantwal (40.3 per cent). The percentage of recovery of PS demand has been 76.5 per cent in the district, around 88 per cent in Sullia and Puttur, 76 per cent in Belthangady, 72.7 per cent in Mangalore and 68.7 per cent in Bantwal. The share of agricultural demand to total agriculture has been 68.3 per cent in the district, the Belthangady, Sullia and Puttur the share being over 75 per cent , in Bantwal, 60 per cent and in Mangalore only 50 per cent. The recovery rate has been 56.3 per cent in the district, the rate in Sullia being above 60 per cent , in Puttur 58 per cent , in Belthangady 53 per cent , 52 per cent in Mangalore and only 49 per cent in Bantwal. The share of SSI demand to total advances has been 35 per cent in the district, over 48 per cent in Puttur, 36 per cent in Mangalore, 21 per cent in Belthangady and Sullia and only 13 per cent in Bantwal. The recovery rate has been 62 per cent in the district, average in Belthangady, Mangalore and Puttur, very high in Sullia (86 per cent) and very low in Bantwal (19 per cent). In OPS, the proportion of demand has been over 70 per cent in Bantwal, 30 per cent in Mangalore and the district, 33 per cent in Puttur, 40 per cent in Sullia and only 23 per cent in Belthangady. The recovery rate has been over 85 per cent in Bantwal, over 75 per cent in Mangalore, Sullia and Puttur, 74.7 per cent in the district and 67.6 per cent in Belthangady.

The share of total IRDP advances has been 51 per cent , higher in Bantwal, (over 62 per cent) and Mangalore (74 per cent), average in Belthangady (38 per cent) lower in Sullia (43 per cent) and lowest in Puttur (36 per cent). The proportion of recovery has been 98.7 per cent , over 28.5 in Belthangady, 77 per cent in Puttur, 57 per cent in Sullia, 46 per cent in Mangalore and only 40 per cent in Bantwal. In Belthangady recovery of old advances has made the recovery rate very high. The share of PMRY demand has been over 30 per cent in all the taluks, same in Puttur (18 per cent), whereas recovery rate has been 62 per cent in Puttur, 51.8 per cent in Sullia and Belthangady, 47 per cent in Bantwal, 46 per cent in the district and 42.7 per cent in Mangalore.

Bankwise Distribution

Bankwise distribution in Bantwal indicates the total demand as Rs. 25.7 crore. The share of PCARD being 7.1 per cent , Canara Bank 17.1 per cent , Vijaya Bank 28.5 per cent , Syndicate Bank 15.4 per cent , Karnataka Bank 14.3 per cent , Corporation Bank and NGB 2.6 per cent each and SBI 2.2 per cent.

In crop cultivation, the outstanding demand has been 23 per cent of advances, Canara Bank, Syndicate Bank, Vijaya Bank and NGB having more than 30 per cent , SBI having 24 per cent , Karnataka Bank having 4.6 per cent and PCARD and Corporation Bank having 0 per cent. The recovery rate has been 84 per cent higher in Karnataka Bank, SBI and Syndicate Bank and lower in others. In minor irrigation the proportion of demand has been 7 per cent higher in PCARD, NGB and Vijaya Bank, the recovery rate being 59 per cent , which is higher in Karnataka Bank. The proportion of SSI has been 6.7 per cent , very high in Karnataka Bank and recovery rate 59.2 per cent higher in Canara and Syndicate banks having higher average.

The proportion of OPS demand has been 29 per cent , Corporation Bank and SBI having higher average, the recovery rate being 71 per cent , higher in NGB, Karnataka and Canara banks. NPS has a share of 14 per cent in demand, higher for Karnataka and Syndicate banks, the recovery rate being 85.6 per cent , higher in Syndicate Bank, Corporation Bank and NGB. The proportion of IRDP has been 1.9 per cent , higher in Syndicate Bank (3.8 per cent) and Vijaya Bank (2.8 per cent). The recovery rate being only 40 per cent. (NGB and Karnataka Bank have higher rates). The proportion of PMRY has been 3 per cent , higher in SBI, Corporation Bank and Vijaya Bank, the recovery rate being 37 per cent higher in Karnataka Bank.

In Belthangady, the total demand outstanding has been Rs. 36.3 crore for 25 branches. Syndicate Bank has 8 branches, Vijaya Bank 6, SCDCC Bank 4, NGB 3, and other banks one each. SCDCC Bank has the largest demand share at 36.4 per cent , followed by Vijaya Bank (21.8 per cent) and Syndicate Bank (19.5 per cent). The other four banks' share has been 23 per cent. The recovery rate has been 76 per cent , higher in SCDCC and Corporation banks. The share of crop cultivation has been 43.9 per cent (higher in SCDCC Bank) and recovery rate 87 per cent (higher in SCDCC and Corporation banks. In minor irrigation, the demand share has been 7.1 per cent (higher in PCARD, NGB, Vijaya Bank), the recovery rate being 52 per cent (higher in SCDCC Bank, Karnataka Bank and NGB). The NFS share is 1.2 per cent (higher in PCARD and Syndicate Bank), the recovery rate being 70 per cent (higher in SCDCC Bank).

The SSI share has been 19 per cent (19.6 per cent in Karnataka Bank) the recovery rate being 65 per cent (higher in SBI and Syndicate Bank). In OPS, Corporation Bank, Karnataka Bank and SBI have a higher share than the taluk average of 18.9 per cent. The recovery rate has been higher in Corporation Bank, SBI and NGB when compared to the taluk average of 67.6 per cent.

The NPS share has been 15.7 per cent (higher in Vijaya Bank and Syndicate Bank), the recovery rate being 78 per cent (higher in Syndicate Bank, Corporation Bank and SCDCC Bank). The IRDP share has been 20.2 per cent (higher in Karnataka Bank) and the rate of recovery has been over 100 per cent. In Karnataka Bank, the recovery has been very high, more than 300 per cent and in SCDCC bank 100 per cent while in others it has been less than 60 per cent. The PMRY share has been 1.8 per cent (Karnataka Bank having 17.6 per cent), the recovery being 52 per cent (higher in THAT bank).

In Mangalore, there are 114 bank branches, Syndicate Bank leading with 26 followed by Canara Bank (22), Vijaya Bank (20), SBI (11), Corporation Bank (11), SBM (4) and others (20). The total demand has been Rs. 321.7 crore with 73 per cent recovery. Syndicate Bank has the largest share, the per branch demand being Rs. 4.3 crore with 66 per cent recovery. Canara Bank also has a higher share at Rs. 4.8 crore per branch with 66 per cent recovery. The per branch average in Corporation Bank has been Rs. 1.2 crore with 73 per cent recovery. The averages in other banks has been around Rs. 0.5 crore. The proportion of crop cultivation has been 1.5 per cent (higher in SBI and Vijaya Bank) and recovery 90 per cent (higher in SBI).

The proportion of minor irrigation has been 0.2 per cent (higher in SBM Vijaya Bank and others) the recovery rate being 66 per cent (higher in other). In NFS, the share has been 1.9 per cent with recovery rate of 74 per cent. Other banks have a higher share in demand and SBM a higher recovery rate. The SSI, the demand share has been 26.7 per cent (very high in Canara Bank at 59.5 per cent and less than 13 per cent in other banks). The recovery rate has been 62.5 per cent (higher in SBM and Syndicate Bank). In OPS, the demand share has been 23.7 per cent higher in SBI, SBM, Corporation and Vijaya banks and recovery rate 75.5 per cent , higher in SBI. The NPS share has been 42.3 per cent (Syndicate Bank having 73 per cent and others less than average) and the recovery rate 79.4 per cent (Corporation Bank, Syndicate bank and SBI having over 80 per cent each). The IRDP share has been only 0.2 per cent higher in Vijaya Bank (1.7 per cent) the recovery rate being 45.6 per cent higher in SBM, Corporation Bank, Canara Bank and others. The PMRY share is 0.7 per cent higher in Vijaya Bank, SBM and Corporation Bank, the recovery rate being 32.7 per cent higher in SBM and Canara Bank.

In Puttur Vijaya Bank has 7 branches, Syndicate Bank 6, SCDCC bank 5, Canara Bank, and NGB 2 each and Corporation Bank, Karnataka Bank, PCARD and SBM one each totally 26 branches. Total demand has been Rs. 69.8 crore, SCDCC Bank having the largest (56.6 per cent) followed by Syndicate Bank (14.1 per cent) and others. The per branch demand has been around Rs. 8 crore in SCDCC Bank followed by PCARD (Rs. 4.2 crore), Canara Bank (Rs. 3.5 crore), Syndicate Bank (Rs. 1.7 crore), NGC (Rs. 1.1 crore), Vijaya Bank (Rs. 0.8 crore), SBM (Rs. 0.7 crore) and Corporation Bank (Rs. 0.1 crore). The average recovery rate has been 88 per cent higher in Karnataka and SCDCC banks. The proportion of crop cultivation is 85.7 per cent (higher in SCDCC Bank at 85.4 per cent), the recovery rate being 96.4 per cent (higher in SCDCC and Corporation banks). The share of minor irrigation has been 4.9 per cent , PCARD, NGB, Vijaya Bank and Syndicate Bank having higher share. The recovery rate has been 70 per cent , higher in SCDCC and Karnataka banks, (10 per cent in the latter). The share of NFS has been 0.7 per cent higher in SBM and Corporation Bank and the recovery rate 71 per cent , higher in Syndicate Bank, SCDCÇ Bank and Vijaya Bank. The SSI share has been only 5.4 per cent (40 per cent in Canara bank), the recovery rate has been 61 per cent , higher in Canara Bank, Syndicate Bank, Vijaya Bank, NGB, Karnataka Bank and PCARD. The average recovery of 76 per cent is excelled in Karnataka Bank, NGB, Corporation Bank, SCDCC Bank and SBM. Syndicate Bank, Karnataka Bank, SBM and

NGB have above average rate of 8 per cent in NPS, where the recovery rate has been 91.4 per cent ; Karnataka Bank has a rate of 106.4 per cent. The IRDP share been 0.5 per cent and that of PMRY 0.3 per cent , Vijaya Bank and Syndicate Bank having higher IRDP share and Syndicate and Vijaya banks having higher PMRY share. The IRDP recovery rate has been 77 per cent (100 per cent in SCDCC Bank while it has been 62 per cent in PMRY, Syndicate Bank having 71 per cent.

In Sullia, the average demand has been Rs. 56.5 with 76.5 per cent recovery. SCDCC bank's share being 59 per cent , which is followed by Canara Bank and Vijaya Bank (11 per cent each) and others. The recovery rate has been 58.4 per cent , SCDCC Bank and others having higher rates. The proportion of crop cultivation has been 61.8 per cent (in SCDCC Bank 88.8 per cent) and the recovery rate 97.6 per cent (in SCDCC Bank 100 per cent). The minor irrigation share has been 4.2 per cent higher in PCARD, Syndicate and Vijaya banks and the recovery rate 67 per cent , SCDCC Bank and NGB each have 100 per cent and Corporation Bank (75.4 per cent). The SSI share has been 1.1 per cent (67.8 per cent in other banks) and the recovery rate 86 per cent , SCDCC Bank and other banks having 100 per cent. The OPS share has been 10.2 per cent very low in SCDCC Bank (3.2 per cent). The recovery rate has been 76.6 per cent higher in NGB and SCDCC Bank. In NPS, the average share has been 12 per cent , Canara and Corporation banks having higher shares with a recovery rate of 78.8 per cent. Both IRDP and PMRY share has been 0.7 per cent in each and the recovery rate 57 per cent in IRDP and 52.3 per cent in PMRY. Syndicate Bank and Vijaya Bank in IRDP and also in PMRY in addition to other banks in the latter have higher shares. The recovery rate has been 100 per cent in SCDCC and PCARD in respect of IRDP demand.

For the five taluks together total demand has been Rs. 510 crore the average per branch being Rs. 2.33 crore. The average recovery rate has been 76.5 per cent. Of the total demand outstanding the share of NPS is 30.9 per cent , OPS (21.2 per cent) followed by crop cultivation (19.7 per cent), SSI (18.2 per cent), minor irrigation (2.1 per cent), NFS (1.6 per cent), PMRY (0.8 per cent), and IRDP (0.4 per cent). The recovery rate has been higher in crop cultivation and IRDP (over 95 per cent in each) average in NFS, OPS and NPS and lower in others.

IRDP, PMRY and Other Government Programmes

If IRDP, PMRY and other government programmes demands are added up the overall share of IRDP have been 15.9 per cent , that of PMRY 5 per cent , 9 per cent , and other government programmes 32.2 per cent in the district. PMRY share is the highest in Bantwal, Mangalore and Sullia. That of other government programmes in Puttur and Belthangady and that of IRDP in Sullia. In Bantwal PMRY share is 59.4 per cent followed by IRDP 22.6 per cent) and other programmes (18 per cent). The share of IRDP has been 100 per cent in PCARD, and 62.6 per cent in NGB. Between 17 to 27 per cent in SBI, Canara Bank, Syndicate Bank and Vijaya Bank, 1.2 per cent in Karnataka Bank and nil in Corporation Bank. PMRY share is more than 60 per cent in SBI, Canara Bank, Corporation Bank, Vijaya Bank and Karnataka Bank; it is 43 per cent in Syndicate Bank and nil in NGB and PCARD. The share of other programmes has been over 35 per cent in Syndicate Bank, around 20 per cent in SBI, around 12 per cent in Vijaya Bank, 8 per cent in Canara Bank and 0 per cent in PCARD.

In Belthangady, the share of other programmes has been 46.6 per cent followed by PMRY (33 per cent) and IRDP (20.4 per cent). IRDP share is higher in SCDCC Bank (100 per cent), Karnataka Bank, NGB and Canara Bank, that of PMRY in SBI and Corporation Bank and that of other programmes in Vijaya Bank. In Mangalore, PMRY share is 672 per cent followed by other programmes 27.2 per cent and IRDP 5.6 per cent. SCDCC Bank in IRDP, Canara Bank, Syndicate Bank, Corporation Bank, Vijaya Bank, Karnataka Bank and ЗBM in PMRY and NGB in other programmes have very high shares.

In Puttur, other programmes have the highest share at 50.3 per cent followed by PMRY (27.2 per cent) and IRDP (22.5 per cent). PCARD and Karnataka Bank have 100 per cent coverage of IRDP while SBM, Canara Bank, Syndicate Bank and Corporation Bank have higher PMRY share while Vijaya Bank and NGB have very higher other programmes shares. The PMRY share in Sullia has been 44.4 per cent followed by IRDP (38 per cent) and other programmes 17.6 per cent SCDCC Bank and PCARD have 100 per cent coverage of IRDP while NGB has 100 per cent coverage of other programmes. Karnataka Bank, Canara Bank and Corporation Bank have very high PMRY share.

In the district of the total deposit accounts of 16.4 lakh, the share of Syndicate Bank has been 20.9 per cent followed by Canara Bank (18.8 per cent), Vijaya bank (16.3 per cent). Corporation bank (11.8 per cent), Karnataka bank (10.5 per cent) other banks (6.9 per cent) SCDCC bank (6.3 per cent), SBI (5 per cent), SBM (1.7 per cent), NGB (1.6 per cent) and PCARD (0.2 per cent). In the total deposit amount of Rs. 3548.7 crore the share of Canara bank has been 18.9 per cent followed by Syndicate bank (17.1 per cent), Corporation bank (14.7 per cent), Vijaya bank (12.2 per cent), other banks (10.1 per cent), Karnataka bank (9.9 per cent), SBI (8.2 per cent), SCDCC bank (5.6 per cent), SBM (2.4 per cent), NGB (0.7 per cent) and PCARD (0.2 per cent).

About 12 per cent of the deposits take advances which number 1.95 lakh accounts. The share of Syndicate bank is the highest (19.4 per cent) followed by Vijaya bank, SCDCC bank, Canara bank, PCARD and others. Total advances amount to Rs. 1904.5 crore indicating a credit deposit ratio of 54 per cent. Per account advance has been Rs. 0.97 crore. In the advance amount the share of Corporation Bank has been the highest (20.2 per cent) followed by Syndicate Bank, Canara bank, other banks, SCDCC bank and others.

The total number of priority sector advances has been 1.08 lakh, Vijaya Bank having the largest share followed by Syndicate Bank, PCARD, Canara Bank, SCDCC bank and others. Total PSA amount has been Rs. 883.3 crore, per account average being Rs. 0.8 csrore. The share of PSA accounts to total advance accounts has been 55 per cent while PSA amounts share has been lower at 46.4 per cent indicating a lower per account advance. In PSA the share of Syndicate Bank has been the highest at 16.5 per cent followed by Canara Bank, other banks, SCDCC Bank, Corporation Bank, Vijaya Bank, SBI, Karnataka Bank, PCARD, NGB and SBM in order of importance. The share of PSA is higher in Canara bank, Vijaya bank, Karnataka bank, NGB Clorporation bank, SCDCC bank and other banks.

Of the total advances share of agriculture has been in total advances over 50 per cent in PCARD and SCDCC bank, close to 49 per cent in SBI, NGB and Vijaya bank and less than 30 per cent in Syndicate bank and less than 8 per cent in Corporation bank, SBM and other banks. The share of SSI has been very high at 48 per cent in Canara bank, Syndicate bank and Karnataka bank (37 per cent in each), SBI and SBM 33 per cent in each and others. The share of NFS has been very high in SBM and NGB and that of OPS in Corporation bank, SBI, Karnataka bank and Vijaya bank. IRDP share has been higher in NGB and Vijaya bank and in PMRY, Vijaya bank and Syndicate bank. The share of PSA in total advance has been over 70 per cent in NGB, over 65 per cent in SCDCC Bank, PCARD Bank and Vijaya Bank, around 52 per cent in Karnataka and Canara banks, around 45 per cent in SBM and Syndicate Bank, 31 per cent in SBI and 25 per cent in Corporation Bank.

The credit deposit ratio is 610 per cent in PCARD, 85 per cent in NGB, 82 per cent in SCDCC bank, 74 per cent in Corporation bank, 70 per cent in SBI and d56 per cent in Syndicate bank. The ratio is very low in SBM and Canara bank (39 per cent in each), Vijaya bank (31 per cent) and Karnataka bank (24.5 per cent).

Per Account Advances

The per account agriculture advance has been Rs. 0.5 lakh for all the banks, Karnataka bank and SCDCC bank having over Rs. 1.5 per SSI advances has been RS. 4.33 lakh the average being over Rs. 7 lakh in SBI, Canara bank and other banks, over Rs. 6 lakh in Karnataka bank and Corporation bank and over Rs. 5 lakh in Syndicate bank. The average NFS advance has been Rs. 0.65 lakh, SBM and Karnataka bank having over rupees one lakh. SBI, Karnataka bank and Corporation bank have over this for an average of Rs. 0.7 lakh. The average IRDP advance has been Rs. 7368, and it is over Rs. 41,000 in SCDCC bank.

In many banks the average has been between 6 to 8 thousand and in PCARD its around Rs. 3000 only. The average PMRY advance has been Rs. 42896, NGB and PCARD not providing any loans. The average is over Rs. 50,000 in SBI and Corporation Bank, over Rs. 45,000 in Canara bank, over Rs. 41,000 in Karnataka bank, SBM and Vijaya bank, around Rs. 37,000 in Syndicate bank and Rs. 26,7000 in SCDCC bank.

When both urban, semi urban and rural branches are considered, there are 38 bank branches in bantwal but only 30 branches participate in the credit plan. In Belthangady its 25 out of 28; in Mangalore it is 114 out of 210; in Puttur it is 26 out of 33 and in Sullia it is 23 out of 24. Perhaps, the urban banks are not participating in the credit plan. For the entire district the total number of bank branches is 333 and only 218 branches participate in the credit plan.

Vijaya bank has the highest share of bank branches (18.9 per cent) followed by Syndicate bank (17.1 per cent), Canara bank (11.7 per cent), Karnataka bank (9.3 per cent), Corporation bank and SCDCC bank (8.4 per cent each), SBI (6.9 per cent), NGB (3.6 per cent), SBM (2.1 per cent) PCARD (1.5 per cent) and other banks (12 per cent). In the credit plan the share of Syndicate bank has been the highest at 23.8 per cent followed by Vijaya bank (22 per cent), Canara bank (14.2 per cent), SBI (6.4 per cent), Corporation bank (6.9 per cent), SCDCC bank (5.5 per cent) Karnataka bank and NGB 3.7 per cent each, SBM 2.3 per cent , PCARD 1.8 per cent and other 9.6 per cent. When compared to the total number of branches the percentage of involvement has been 60 per cent in SBI, 71 per cent in SBM, 79 per cent in Canara bank, 91 per cent in Syndicate bank, 76 per cent in Vijaya bank, 53 per cent in Corporation bank, 26 per cent in Karnataka bank, 67 per cent in NGB, 80 per cent in PCARD, 43 per cent in SCDCC bank and 52 per cent in other banks. The rural and semi urban/urban distribution of different bank branches is presented in table.

The share of SBI in 1988-90 credit plan has been 4.8 per cent , which declined to 4.3 per cent in 2000, that of SBM has increasing from 0.8 to 1 per cent in the period. The share of Canara bank has shown an increase from 16.7 to 19 per cent while Syndicate bank's share has declined from 33.2 to 24.8 per cent. There has been a decline in Vijaya bank also from 115 to 5.7 per cent. The share of Corporation bank has increased from 8.3 to 11.2 per cent while that of Karnataka bank improved from 4.9 to 7.8 per cent. SCDCC bank's share increased from 6.9 to 18.3 per cent while NGB's share declined from 4.1 to 3.5 per cent and that of KSFC's increasing from 4.1 to 4.5 per cent.

Credit Plans

During 1988-90, the share of agriculture and allied sectors in term loan has been 27.8 per cent , the share of SSI being 35.6 per cent and that of tertiary sector 36.5 per cent. In agriculture crop banks, irrigation and allied sectors had a large share. According to 2002-03 credit plan the percentage of outlay on agriculture and allied sectors has shown a decline to 19 per cent. The share of rural artisans and SSI has been 22 per cent and that of trade and services 26 per cent , having 33 per cent for the non-priority sector.

According to blockwise credit plan for 2002-03 total number of crop loans in the district has been around 10,700 with an average loan of Rs. 91000 . Mangalore and Bantwal together account for over 60 per cent. Of the accounts and the average loan amount has been higher in Sullia (Rs. 236,000) followed by Puttur and Belthangady. The total number of minor irrigation units has been around 4600. Puttur and Belthangady accounting for about 50 per cent. The average loan amount has been Rs. 36,000 higher only in Mangalore. Land development units has been 2100, Puttur and Bantwal having larger share. The average loan amount has been Rs. 40,000, higher in Bantwal. The number farm mechanization units have been 422 with an average loan amount of Rs. 100,000. Mangalore, Puttur and Sullia had a higher share of the units, the loan amount being higher in Belthangady and Sullia. The number of plantation and Horticulture units has been 1600 with an average loan amount of Rs. 29,000. Belthangady's share was more than 50 per cent , Mangalore having a very investment (Rs. 1.5 lakh). In other agriculture and animal husbandry including fisheries, the total number of accounts has been around 3600 with an assistance ranging from Rs. 15,000 to 1.3 lakh. Mangalore has a very high share in these areas. This is so in respect of allied sector as well. In the agriculture sector total number of units have been about 24000, the share of Mangalore being 28 per cent , that of Bantwal 22 per cent , Puttur 20 per cent , Belthangady 18 per cent and Sullia 12 per cent. The average loan amount has been Rs. 0.65 lakh, slightly higher in Puttur and double in Sullia. Whereas in the other three taluks it has been less than Rs. 0.5 lakh.

The total number of SSI units has been 3500, Mangalore accounting for 70 per cent of that with an average assistance of Rs. 5.3 lakh, higher in Mangalore here also. The number of OPS units has been 22,000, Mangalore accounting for 63 per cent with an assistance of Rs. 1.3 lakh. The total number of priority accounts has been around 50,000 with an average loan amount of Rs. 1.13 lakh and that of non priority sector 52,600 with an average loan amount of Rs. 0.53 lakh. In the total priority sector accounts the share of Mangalore has been 46.3 per cent with an above average loan of Rs. 1.61 lakh, followed by Bantwal at 19.5 per cent and a lower loan amount of Rs. 0.47 lakh, Puttur 14.7 per cent with a loan amount of Rs. 0.91 lakh, Belthangady 11.5 per cent with a lower loan amount of Rs. 0.53 lakh, lastly Sullia 8 per cent with a higher loan average of

Rs. 1.25 lakh. In the non-priority accounts share of Mangalore has been 70.7 per cent with an average loan amount of Rs. 0.62 lakh, above the district average of Rs. 0.53 lakh. Next in importance is Belthangady with 11.9 per cent share but having a very low loan amount of Rs. 0.16 lakh followed by Puttur (10.9 per cent) with a lower loan amount of Rs. 0.26 lakh, Bantwal (4.8 per cent) with a higher loan amount of Rs. 0.62 lakh and lastly by Sullia (1.8 per cent) with a higher loan average of Rs. 0.64 lakh. The total number of priority and non-priority sector has been above one lakh with an average loan amount of Rs. 0.82 lakh. Mangalore has the largest share at 58.8 per cent followed by Puttur (12.7 per cent), Bantwal (12 per cent), Belthangady (11.7 per cent) and Sullia (4.8 per cent). The average loan amount has been higher in Sullia and Mangalore, lower in Puttur and Bantwal and very low in Belthangady.

Of the total accounts, the share of women has been 12.6 per cent with a lower loan amount of Rs. 0.38 lakh. The share has been higher in Belthangady (32.9 per cent) and Bantwal (18.8 per cent) but the loan amount lower than the average. The coverage of women has been only 5.2 per cent in Sullia, 6.1 per cent in Puttur and 9.3 per cent in Mangalore. While the loan amount has been higher than the average in Puttur and Mangalore its lower in Sullia. The share of SGSY has been 1.1 per cent and all taluks except Mangalore having a higher share. The average loan amount has been Rs. 0.28 lakh higher in Puttur, above average in Belthangady and Sullia and below average in Mangalore and Bantwal. The share of PMRY has been 0.9 per cent higher in Mangalore and lower in Belthangady. The average loan amount in all the taluks is Rs. 0.67 lakh. The share of special programmes has been 5.9 per cent slightly higher in Puttur and Sullia and lower in Belthangady. The average loan amount has been 0.38 lakh higher in Belthangady and Sullia, average in Puttur and below average in Mangalore and Bantwal.

The Macro Picture

In state of Karnataka, total number of bank credit accounts in 1992-93 has been 49.2 lakh with an outstanding of Rs. 9293.4 crore. The share of agriculture in accounts has been 44.3 per cent , industry 4.7 per cent , transport operations 1 per cent , professional and other service 6.7 per cent , personal loans 13.8 per cent , trade 14.2 per cent , finance 0.03 per cent , miscellany 15.3 per cent , artisans and village industries 1.9 per cent and other SSIs 2.1 per cent. The change in share during 1998-99 when there was a decline in to 43.3 per cent lakh has been agriculture (38.5 per cent), industry (8.3 per cent), transport operations (1.5 per cent) professional and other services (3.7 per cent), personal loans (27.3 per cent) trade (10.2 per cent), finance 0.005 per cent , miscellany (10.4 per cent), artisans and village industries 1.6 per cent and other SSIs 5.4 per cent.

Of the credit outstanding the share of agriculture has been 21.5 per cent in 1992-93, industry's share being 42.4 per cent , transport operations 0 per cent , professional and other services 4.1 per cent , personal loans 10.9 per cent , trade 6 per cent , finance 3 per cent , miscellany 6.7 per cent , artisans 0.5 per cent and other SSIs 10.8 per cent. During 1998-99 when the credit increased upto 25527.8 crore, the share of agriculture has been 16.9 per cent , industry share being 41.2 per cent , transport operation 2 per cent , professional and other services 4 per cent , personal loans 14.2 per cent , trade 9 per cent , finance 4.2 per cent miscellany 8.3 per cent , artisan and village industries 0.5 per cent and other SSIs 8.5 per cent. This indicate that agriculture share has declined, also that of industries and SSIs while that of professional and other services, personal loans, trade and finance have increased substantially Karnataka's share in deposits outstanding increased from 5 per cent in 1992-93 to 5.5 per cent in 1998-99.

The Reserve Bank of India is to switch over to risk based supervision of banks during this year. If banks should not fail corrective action has to be taken by supervisors as noted by Basel Committee once capital is less than threshold level compulsory quantitative triggers in relation to capital levels have to be followed for recapitalization. Restrictions involve limiting new acquisitions and restricting interest rates on deposits. When capital level is very low mergers of closures are allowed. In 1999 a system of prompt corrective action has been introduced wherein the responsibility of bank supervisors in identifying problem banks and monitoring the behaviour of troubled banks are resorted to. The intervention can be structured or discretionary. In the risk based supervision started in June 2001, development of risk profile, designing customized supervisory action plan based on risk profile, supervision to target high risk areas and quality assurance and enforcement are emphasized. For this the banks have to set up comprehensive risk management system, adopt risk focused internal audit system, upgrade management information system, set up dedicated complaints units and tackle issues related to human resource and skill development. Banks have to improve the risk management in order to prepare contingency plans to measure their ability to withstand liquidity crises and to estimate future volatility in values of securities. Some banks have set up risk management committees (RBI 2002). Asset rehabilitation involves swapping impaired assets for cash or bonds at market prices improve capital adequacy and liquidity. Deposit insurance will protect especially small depositors who will not be in a position to monitor the soundness of the banks.

Income of scheduled commercial banks as a percentage of total assets have declined from 10.4 in 1999-2000 to 10.2 per cent in 2000-01 and further to 9.84 per cent in 2001-02. The share of interest income in 2000-01 but declined to 84 per cent in 2001-02. The share of expenditure has declined from 9.74 to 97 and further to 9.1 per cent in 2001-02. There has been a decline in operating expenses including wage bill from 2.5 to 2.2 per cent. Though during 2000-01 it went up to 2.64 per cent. The interest spread has increased to 2.85 in 2000-01 but declined to 2.57 per cent during the succeeding year. There has been an increase in the share of operating profit from 1.66 to 1.94 per cent though in 2000-01 it went down to 1.53 per cent. The net profit as percentage of total assets which was 0.66 per cent in 1999-02 declined to 0.49 per cent in 2000-01 however increasing to 0.75 per cent in 2001-02. The share of income has been slightly higher in the nationalized banks but lower in the state bank group, the interest spread slightly higher in the former and net profit higher in the state bank group. For the nationalized banks the interest spread increased from 2.66 to 2.9 declining to 2.74 per cent in the terminal year. The spread increased from 2.76 to 2.79 declining to 2.71 in the state bank group. The share of net profit declined from 0.44 to 0.33 per cent in the case of nationalized banks, increasing to 0.69 per cent in 2001-02. There was a steep decline in the share in the state bank group from 0.8 to 0.55 in 2001 increasing to 0.77 per cent in the succeeding year.

The old private banks have a higher income share and also net profit though the interest spread is smaller. The new private banks however have lower income share, lower interest rates and also lower net profit share. Foreign banks have a larger income share, a higher interest spread and a higher net profit level. As on March 2002 the share of nationalized banks in total assets has been 46 per cent but in net profit it has 41.9 per cent. The share of state bank group in total assets has been 29.3 per cent and in net profit 29.8 per cent. The share of old private banks in total assets has been 6.1 per cent the share in net profit being 8.7 per cent. New private banks have a larger asset share (11.4 per cent) but a smaller profit share (6.7 per cent). The foreign banks have a share of 7.2 per cent in assets and 12.9 per cent in profit indicating a relatively higher profit performance when compared to nationalized and new private banks (RBI 2002). Total credit deployment in 2001-02 to the priority sector has been 38.9 per cent (agriculture 16.5 per cent , SSI 2.2 per cent and OPS 20.2 per cent), medium and large scale industry 17.7 per cent , whole sale trade 4.9 per cent and other sectors 38.5 per cent (housing 11.6 per cent , NBFCs 3.4 per cent , consumer durables 2.7 per cent and etc). In the industry sector power, roads and ports, drugs and pharmaceuticals, textiles and iron and steel have a larger credit share. There has been a decline in lending to capital market by all the banks. Corporation bank, SBI, federal bank NDFC bank, Karnataka bank, Vijaya bank and UTI bank have experienced increased in their share prices in 2001-02 while bank of Baroda, ICICI bank and Dena bank have experienced a decline. Of the total net profit of Rs. 8301 crore in 2001-02 the share of state bank group has been 41.5 per cent when compared to 51.5 per cent in the preceding year amongst the PSBs indicating a better performance of the nationalized banks in the terminal year.

The gross NPAs of SCBs increased from Rs. 637.4 billion in 2001 to Rs. 709 billion in d2001-02. There was an increase in net NPAs from Rs. 324.6 to Rs. 355.5 billion. The PSBs account for about 80 per cent of all NPAs. However ratio of gross NPA to gross advances demand from 11.4 to 10.4 per cent in 2001-02 and as percentage of net advances at NPA declined from 6.2 to 5.5 per cent. The share of gross NPA in total assets declined from 4.9 to 4.6 per cent. The NPAs of PSBs increased marginally in spite of recoveries while in foreign banks recoveries exceeded additions. In the new private banks there was addition NPA because of mergers. The share of gross NPA to total assets has declined from 6.7 per cent in 1999 to 4.9 per cent in 2002. In the case of PSBs, the decline has been from 5.8 to 5.2 per cent in old private sector banks and from 3.1 to 2.4 per cent in foreign banks. While the ratio increased from 2.3 to 3.9 per cent in the case of new private sector banks. The decline in net NPA in the PSBs has been from 3.1 to 3.4 per cent , in old private sector banks from 3.6 to 3.2 per cent and in foreign banks from 1.1 to 0.8 per cent , while in the new private sector banks the increase has been from 1.6 to 2.1 per cent. In the case of PSBs priority sector accounted for 44.5 per cent of NPAs, public sector contributing to 2 per cent and non-priority sector 53.5 per cent. In the case of private sector banks the shares have been 21.81, 0.3 and 77.9 per cent respectively.

In the PSBs the share of standard assets increased from 84.1 per cent in 1999 to 88.9 per cent in 2002 the increase in the old private sector banks being 86.9 to 89 per cent and in foreign banks 92.4 to 94.5 per cent while in new private sector banks the decline has been from 93.8 to 91.1 per cent while there has been a decline in the share of substandard, doubtful and loss assets. In PSBs there has been an increase in the share of doubtful assets in the private sector and foreign banks. 3 PSBs, 5 private sector banks and 14 foreign banks had over 10 per cent of NPAs. More than 80 per cent SCBs have over 10 per cent of capital to risk weighted assets ratio, some banks have also returned capital to the government of India and many PSBs raised subordinated debts to augment capital private sector banks also raising equity capital along with subordinated debt.

Table 5.1: Performance of Scheduled Commercial Banks (as per cent to total)

Bank	*NetInt. Inc*	*Emp/ Sal*	*Tot Exp*	*Net Pro*	*Cap*	*Tot Dep*	*Tot Lia*	*Tot Adv*	*Tot Asts*
PSBs									
Canara	5.8	5.2	6.0	8.9	3.8	6.7	6.2	6.9	6.2
SBI	28.7	23.8	27.3	26.9	3.5	28.5	30.1	25.1	30.1
Syndicate	3.5	3.8	3.9	3.0	3.1	3.0	2.7	3.1	2.7
Vijaya	1.5	1.4	1.6	1.6	2.2	1.5	1.4	1.3	1.4
Corporation	2.1	1.0	1.5	4.5	1.0	2.0	2.1	2.3	2.1
Total (Rs. bil)	317	216	264	84	150	9488	11564	4808	11565
Private Banks									
Global Trust	1.8	2.4	4.6	2.1	4.6	3.9	2.8	2.7	2.8
HDFC	12.9	7.2	11.2	15.4	10.8	10.7	9.1	6.0	9.1
ICICI	12.1	9.7	16.7	13.4	36.8	19.4	39.6	41.1	39.6
Karnataka	2.9	5.9	3.5	4.7	0.5	4.2	3.0	3.0	3.0
Total (Rs. bil)	48.9	15.2	37.3	19.3	26.2	1653	2627	1144	2627

Contd...

Table 5.1–Contd...

Bank	*NetInt. Inc*	*Emp/ Sal*	*Tot Exp*	*Net Pro*	*Cap*	*Tot Dep*	*Tot Lia*	*Tot Adv*	*Tot Asts*
Foreign Banks									
ABN-Amro	9.8	8.7	8.5	6.7	5.5	7.8	6.9	9.6	6.9
B of America	4.1	3.7	2.8	4.5	0.1	3.0	4.8	6.3	4.8
Citibank	22.7	15.5	23.9	17.0	5.2	24.3	20.1	24.4	20.1
Mizuho	0.2	0.3	0.3	0.3	2.2	0.3	0.3	0.5	0.3
Stanchart	20.0	13.6	14.2	21.4	11.6	11.6	17.6	19.4	17.6
Total (Rs. bil)	**35.5**	**10.5**	**31.7**	**19.2**	**32.2**	**627**	**1072**	**466**	**1072**

Source: Business India, Best Banks supplement, September 2002

Table 5.2: Performance of Major Banks (per cent to total assets)

CAPITAL ADEQUACY

Bank	*C A Ratio %*	*Dep/Cap %*	*Adv/Asset %*	*Govt Sec as % to Invas*	*Govt Sec % to asset*
OCBC Bank	192.1	0.01	07.3	61.6	12.9
Toronto Dom Bank	173.3	0.00	32.5	99.5	11.7
Corporation Bank	017.9	9.94	44.4	77.5	32.4
HDFC Bank	013.9	10.0	28.6	44.1	22.3
Karnataka Bank	013.0	16.1	44.0	81.2	36.3
Vijaya Bank	012.3	22.3	38.4	75.6	34.5
Syndicate Bank	012.1	20.3	46.9	81.9	30.7
Canara Bank	011.9	18.9	45.9	71.4	21.0
ICICI Bank	011.6	12.3	45.2	63.3	21.8
SBI	011.2	18.4	34.7	80.6	38.6

RESOURCES DEPLOYED

Bank	*Asset Rs. Crore*	*Liquid % of Asset*	*Invest % of Asset*	*Advan % of Asset*	*Fix. K % of Asset*	*Others % of Asset*
State Bank of India	348229	18.65	41.68	34.9	0.69	4.29
ICICI	104110	12.28	34.47	45.18	4.07	3.99
Canara Bank	72211.4	17.31	32.16	45.87	0.91	3.75
Syndicate Bank	31756.2	9.9	37.51	46.87	1.07	4.66
Corporation bank	24293.5	8.94	41.83	44.39	1.49	3.36
HDFC Bank	23787.4	14.54	50.46	28.64	1.56	4.79
Vijaya Bank	16144.5	10.25	45.59	38.38	1.03	4.75
Karnataka Bank	7762.89	8.28	44.66	44.02	0.96	2.07

Asset Quality

Bank	Net NPA % to net Adv	Adv % to Asset	Adv % to GTH	Inv % to Asset	Adv % to Yield	Inv % to Yield	Inv % to GTH
Mitsubushi	0	54.36	36.46	23.74	10.9	9.54	54
Bank of America	0.18	56.79	-16.61	25.74	9.68	9.07	3.1
Corporation Bank	0.31	44.39	27.81	41.83	10.14	10.05	-25.5
Canara Bank	3.89	45.87	19.02	32.16	10.27	11.18	8.28
Syndicate Bank	4	46.87	13.48	37.51	11.43	10.75	12.9
ICICI Bank	4.7	45.18	568.92	34.47	2.85	5.6	338
State Bank of India	5.66	34.69	6.35	41.6	9.44	10.65	18.1
Karnataka Bank	5.9	44.02	20.84	44.66	12.46	10.17	24.4
Vijaya Bank	6.02	38.38	8.33	45.59	11.98	11.56	25.4

Management Quality

Bank	Composite score	Cred/dep %	NP to Eplm % Rs. lakh	Busi per empl Rs. lakh	ROA NW %
Bank of America	51	153.9	32	1769	14.29
Deutsche Bank	40	76.24	28	986.2	18.4
Corporation Bank	20	58.53	3	290.4	21.62
Canara Bank	19	51.74	2	214.9	23.58
Karnataka Bank	19	48.81	2	247.2	22.98
ICICI bank	18	146.59	5	486.5	6.53
Vijaya Bank	16	42.21	1	169.4	20.75
Syndicate Bank	15	52.14	1	155.1	19.09
State Bank of India	14	44.65	1	173	16.95

Earnings Quality

Bank	Net profit (Rs.Cr)	EPS GTH%	Spread %	O1 NII%	NP TAA%
State Bank of India	2431.62	51.67	2.61	45.97	0.73
Corporation Bank	373.18	19.21	2.65	68.58	0.34
CITI Bank	325	52.27	3.76	99.5	0.43
HDFC Bank	297.04	22.39	2.65	52.96	1.51
Syndicate Bank	251	6.81	3.49	24.93	0.84
Vijaya Bank	131	98.74	3.01	38.89	0.86
Karnataka Bank	91	102.22	1.81	172.1	1.26
Canara Bank	741	160	2.52	78.47	1.07

Liquidity

Bank	Liquid/ AST%	G-SEC/ AST%	A SEC/ AST%
KBC Bank	80.4	12.05	0
OCBC Bank	62.37	12.93	0
State Bank of India	18.65	33.61	6.24
Canara Bank	17.31	22.95	3.54
ICICI Bank	12.28	21.83	0.51
Vijaya Bank	10.25	34.48	6.58
Syndicate Bank	9.9	30.7	3.66
Corporation Bank	8.94	32.43	4.63
Karnataka Bank	8.28	36.26	3.46

Source: Business India, Super Banks Special, 2002

Table 5.3: Performance Indicators as % to total assets

Bank Group	*Net Profit*		*Interest*		*Ope expen*		*Wage*		*Provi*		*Spread*		*Income*		*Expend*	
	I	*II*	*I*	*II*	*I*	*II*	*I*	*II*	*I*	*II*	*I*	*II*	*I*	*II*	*I*	*II*
All	0.82	0.66	9.3	9.0	2.6	2.5	1.8	1.9	1.0	1.0	3.0	2.7	10.8	10.4	10.0	9.7
SBI (8)	1.06	0.80	9.1	8.7	2.7	2.5	2.0	1.8	1.0	0.9	3.1	2.8	10.7	10.1	9.6	9.3
Nationalized (19)	0.62	0.44	9.1	9.1	2.7	2.6	1.9	1.9	0.7	0.9	2.8	2.7	10.3	10.3	9.7	9.8
PSBs (27)	0.77	0.57	9.1	8.9	2.7	2.5	1.9	1.8	0.8	0.9	2.9	2.7	10.4	10.2	9.7	9.6
Old Private (24)	0.81	0.84	10.0	9.6	2.3	2.2	1.4	1.4	1.2	1.0	2.6	2.3	11.7	11.3	10.9	10.4
New Private (8)	1.55	0.97	9.3	7.5	1.8	1.4	0.3	0.3	1.3	1.0	2.2	1.9	11.7	9.2	10.1	8.2
Foreign (42)	0.97	1.17	10.4	9.9	3.0	3.2	1.0	1.0	2.9	2.1	3.9	3.8	13.4	12.5	12.4	11.3

I= 1997-98 II= 1999-2002

Source: adapted from Business India (2002) and Das (2002)

Table 5.4: Bank Performance in Dakshina Kannada

	1998-99	*1999-00*	*2000-01*	*2001-02*
Bank Branches	322	333	338	333
Total Adv(Rs.cr)	1304.6	1626.8	1868.1	2129
Priority sector %	43.3	46.4	49.6	43.8
Agrl as % PSA	34.8	30	35.7	29.9
SSI as % PSA	33.1	36.1	31	32
Small road +Water Tr	8.9	7.7	10.6	9.5
Retail trade	7.3	10.2	9.8	8.6
Small Business	4.3	3.8	5.6	4.6
Prof +Self Empl	4.3	3.5	6.1	6.1
Education	1.2	1	2	2
Weaker housing	5.1	7.6	8.6	6.6
Cons.Loans	1	0.1	0.3	0.3
Credit Deposit Ratio	45	45	46	46
Direct Agrl% Total Adv.	15	12	11	8
DRI as %	0.04	0.03	0.02	0.02
Weaker SEC %	8	8	7	7
Advance per branch(Rs. cr)	4.1	4.9	5.5	6.4

Source: Syndicate Bank, District Credit Plan for D.K District, 2002

Table 5.5 : Bankwise service area recovery & outstanding (Sept 99) in % age

Item/Bank		*SBI*	*Canara*	*Corp*	*Syndi*	*Vijaya*	*Karn*	*Netrav*	*ARD+*
Total Adv									
	A/c	1.8	11.2	8.5	24.0	20.0	5.6	3.1	12.8
	Amount	2.0	11.8	11.1	25.8	11.2	9.9	1.3	14.8
Total Priority sector Advance									
	A/c	56.0	59.7	41.4	53.9	68.3	30.7	78.7	84.4
	Amount	53.1	54.6	35.5	48.3	56.9	33.9	77.4	96.4
Total Adv. for Agriculture									
	A/c	15.4	19.0	9.7	26.0	43.4	4.8	57.9	38.2
	Amount	12.2	11.3	5.6	13.6	27.3	4.0	41.7	39.9
Total Adv to SSI Sector									
	A/c	7.6	12.0	3.0	8.5	3.8	4.3	13.2	35.4
	Amount	11.1	23.2	7.6	22.9	7.6	15.2	19.4	37.0
Total Advance to OPS									
	A/c	33.0	28.7	28.7	19.4	21.1	21.6	7.6	10.8
	Amount	29.8	20.1	22.3	11.8	22.0	14.7	16.3	58.6
Total Advance Under IRDP									
	A/c	3.0	5.1	5.9	10.4	14.3	1.1	18.4	0.4
	Amount	0.3	0.5	0.5	1.0	3.2	0.1	4.2	0.3
Total Advance Under PMRY									
	A/c	3.1	2.1	1.8	1.5	2.2	1.4	0	0
	Amount	1.9	1.6	1.1	1.1	3.0	0.7	0	0
Others									
	A/c	37.9	33.1	50.9	34.2	15.2	66.8	2.9	15.2
	Amount	44.7	43.3	62.9	49.6	36.9	65.3	18.4	0

Source: Syndicate Bank, Lead Bank data

Table 5.6: PSA and other advance ranges in different taluks

BANTWAL

	0	> 10 lakh			5.1 - 10 lakh			2.1 - 5 lakh			1.1 - 2 lakh			0.5 -1 lakh		< 0.5 lakh	
	No	No	Av.dd	I.R	No	Av.dd	I.R	No	Av.dd	I.R	No	Av.dd	I.R	No	I.R.	No	Av.dd
CL, P/H	16	15	7589	80.52	1	567	73.5	2	315	72.4	-	-	3	29.02	9	4.9	20
MI	1	2	1463	70.59	6	622	58.4	4	327	52.4	148	73.04	2	100	4	23	88
LDFM	18	5	2194	72.09	2	755	67.7	6	116	27	55	35.55	3	35.86	7	6.5	24
Att DD	36	0			0	-124	7	0	-	-	7 37	12.17	6	20.28	20	3.3	9.9
SMY,NFS	17	1	3055	93.19	4	332	40.8	7	77.9	24.1	103	57.48	5	35.5	10	4.5	12
SSI	15	3	5204	46.14	1	503	96.8	1	489	48.7	184	54.89	2	88.3	0		
OPS	2	19	3103	75.09	0			2	425	99.8				0		0	
NPS	6	9	4058	89.72	5	904	90.9	3	419	95.7				0		0	
IRDP	10	0			0			5	342	70.3	173	81.87	2	36.82	3	22	37
PMRY	22	0			1	625	62.1	8	85.2	16.3	58	34.4	4	31.67	6	10	27
	143	54			20			38						27		59	

Contd.........

Table Contd.........

MANGALORE

	0	> 10 lakh			5.1 - 10 lakh			2.1 - 5 lakh			1.1 - 2 lakh			0.5 -1 lakh		< 0.5 lakh	
	No	No	Av.dd	I.R	No	Av.dd	I.R	No	Av.dd	I.R	No	Av.dd	I.R	No	I.R.	No	Av.dd
CL, P/H	155	12	462	14.3	4	366.4	47.27	4	156.6	35.67	35.8	18.23	4	36.51	21	1.4	4.23
MI	78	2	150	77.32	0	5	341	73.67	110	68.18	3	69.4	15	20	66.6		
LDFM	174	1	1752	88.53	5	276.9	29.5	5	133.3	28.56	61.8	29.5	8	19.87	11	3.1	15.3
Agrl DD	330	7	608	10.51	3	695.7	47.62	17	71.67	10.77	92.7	35.83	5	16.19	48	12	4.15
SMYINFS	343	10	1981	14.7	8	194.8	21.55	16	62.37	12.69	73.9	36.6	11	20.69	21	3	10.8
SSI	31	3	3575	97.7	0	-	-	1	42196	77.18	1105	65.29	65	5.75	0	-	
NPS	17	4	698519	92.41	1	93580	85.08	5	35189	90.47	1424	84.78	66	74.33	0		
IRDP	79	1	1190	47.9	1	655	57.25	3	283.7	53.64	142	72.9	1	90.65	9	23	
PMRY	90	1	1094	44.97	11	656.9	35.45	29	21.2	3.42	13.3	5.52	19	6.27	35	1.4	4.32

Contd........

Table Contd.........

BELTHANGADY

	0	> 10 lakh			5.1 - 10 lakh			2.1 - 5 lakh			1.1 - 2 lakh			0.5 -1 lakh		< 0.5 lakh	
	No	No	Av.dd	I.R	No	Av.dd	I.R	No	Av.dd	I.R	No	Av.dd	I.R	No	I.R.	No	Av.dd
CL, P/H	6	11	4250.9	79.84	3	477.3	52.56	5	134	24.7	81	41.25	3	37.75	4	12	80
MI	1	1	1871	77.28	11	756.4	70.11	3	330	49.13	140	75.71	0	1	48	75	
LDFM	13	3	5403.2	60.82	5	251	31.18	3	261.7	63.08	61.2	24.13	2	60.09	5	8.9	35.4
Att DD	46	1	47120	100	0	-	-	4	218.4	60.09	148	66.78	3	65.49	12	4.9	20.6
Ald smy nfs	48	5	1613.4	33.13	2	652.5	80.73	1	267	26.22	132	76.02	4	64.78	10	3.5	9.89
SSI	8	2	1319.5	93.8	3	714.3	88.46	1	294	66.67	171	74.36	0	2	19	31.8	
OPS	1	16	2869.3	85.51	0	1	366	93.44	0	0							
NPS	4	10	3545	91.97	2	722.5	98.38	2	413.5	92.72	0	0					
IRDP	2	0			1	510	74.51	8	368.6	65.21	134	58.48	2	97.62	2	37	64.3
PMRY	20	0			0	10	59.19	16.51	145	71.86	1	26.32	1	7	85.7		

Contd.........

Table Contd.........

PUTTUR

	0	> 10 lakh			5.1 - 10 lakh			2.1 - 5 lakh			1.1 - 2 lakh			0.5 -1 lakh		< 0.5 lakh	
	No	*No*	*Av.dd*	*I.R*	*No*	*Av.dd*	*I.R*	*No*	*Av.dd*	*I.R*	*No*	*Av.dd*	*I.R*	*No*	*I.R.*	*No*	*Av.dd*
CL, P/H	10	11	18862	92.07	2	852.5	72.39	3	172.8	49.45	131	73.9	1	51.47	6	8.4	27.9
MI	1	6	1464.3	70.62	3	802	90.29	4	318.3	80.99	152	80.89	0	2	20	100	
LDFM	9	0			8	159.2	20.72	7	99.33	23.5	75.7	39.2	2	76.17	6	6.6	31.5
Att DD	46	1	1926	65.99	0	2	359.5	90.59	73.9	35.3	8	34.49	11	5.1	20.6		
SMY,Nfs	29	3	1446	49.93	3	444.8	34.06	4	157.8	37.26	116	64.43	7	31.85	4	7.1	45
SSI	8	1	5084	30.74	1	505	0.59	3	296.7	86.03	176	53.12	1	68.75	1	25	100
OPS	1	13	4228.9	90.99	3	790	71.86	1	441	49.21	0	0					
NPS	3	9	7624.6	84.78	1	942	92.36	2	311.5	51.51	163	72.56	0	0			
IRDP	2	0			2	626.5	71.28	4	338.8	60.1	147	69.54	3	91.23	1	49	100
PMRY	15	0			1	95.9	49.32	5	109.6	27.66	58	20.25	6	20.25	4	43	39.5

Contd.........

Table Contd.........

SULLIA

	0	> 10 lakh			5.1 - 10 lakh			2.1 - 5 lakh			1.1 - 2 lakh			0.5 -1 lakh		< 0.5 lakh	
	No	No	Av.dd	I.R	No	Av.dd	I.R	No	Av.dd	I.R	No	Av.dd	I.R	No	I.R.	No	Av.dd
CL, P/H	8	11	26462	92.89	3	539	3.17	1	249	73.9	110	74.83	1	0	1	5	100
MI	0	5	1506	81.99	2	744.5	100	3	407.7	67.16	151	76.18	0	0			
LDFM	10	6	441.79	28.78	3	514.7	53.79	5	126.6	28.93	126	100	1	70.27	2	19	75
Att DD	38	1	1702	100	0	3	384	74.89	124	62.34	0	0	12	283	11		
SMY,Nfs	20	2	1248	91.17	0	9	108.3	28.82	114	49.27	3	45.67	6	6.1	27.2		
SSI	7	0			1	862	28.42	2	345.5	51.82	1	100	3	27	59.8		
OPS	0				11	2431.1	80.09	1	631	73.22	1	450	70	1	100	0	
NPS	1	7	5038.7	75	2	683.5	94.83	3	382	88.24	1	60.53	0				
IRDP	2	1	1208	42.3	1	602	34.39	5	388.3	83.46	194	73.95	2	40.61	1	47	55.3
PMRY	12	1	1094	56.76	1	675	48.89	3	193	42.41	75.3	33.98	5	31.32	2	17	53.1

Source: Syndicate Bank, Lead District Bank data

Table 5.7: Talukwise demand position

Taluk	*Bantwal*	*Belthangady*	*M'lore*	*Puttur*	*Sullia*	*D.K.(mil)*
Demand	4.3	4	79.3	6.2	6.2	62.64
% Recovery	85.2	88.9	87.2	90.8	94.6	87.8
% O.D	14.8	11.1	12.8	9.2	5.4	12.2
CL-dd	16.5	7.13	4	30.48	41.94	11.14
% to PSA	42.8	20.13	5.61	55.16	74.24	—
% recover	94.2	86.7	84.92	98.59	98.58	96.46
MI -DD	18	23.1	10.8	26	22.1	0.77
LD	33.4	22.2	12.7	10.7	21	0.63
FM	7.8	53.6	9.8	13.8	15	0.46
Hort	3.5	11.4	66.8	10.7	7.6	0.26
AH	2.7	75.6	13.5	3.2	5	1.03
Fish	0	1.5	88.1	10.4	0	0.29
ALD	1.6	6.5	83.8	4.4	3.7	2.09
NFS	13.1	27.1	47.9	9.7	2.2	0.72
SSI	1.7	0.5	96.9	0.7	0.2	16.13
OPS	11	8.5	64.8	10.6	5.1	8.64
NPS	1.2	1	94.8	2	1	56.91
IRDP	—	—	—	—	—	0.29
PMRY	—	—	—	—	—	0.52
Others	—	—	—	—	—	0.1

Table 5.7.1: Outstanding Advances (D.K-1999-2000)

Part I

	Total Deposits		Total Advances		Total Priority Sector Adv		Total Agrs Advances		Agrl Direct		Agrl Indirect	
	Lakhs	Per/Rs	Lakhs	Per/Rs	000	Per/Rs	000	Per/Rs	000	Rs	000	Rs
Bantwal	1.406	11182	0.172	43547	13.96	45336	7.58	37145	7.33	26145	0.25	362435
Belthangady	0.846	10997	0.107	54348	7.56	50581	4.25	39274	3.76	39352	0.48	38661
Mangalore	7.112	22748	0.683	124981	23.18	146261	3.65	81867	3.62	46186	0.01	4E+06
Puttur	1.382	11390	0.17	50963	191.25	3314	188.25	2068	187.06	710	1.19	215912
Sullia	0.386	11418	0.01	51884	7.96	31707	5.28	31464	2.55	31963	2.74	31000
D.K.	11.138	18593	1.229	91421	243.9	21692	209.01	6232	204.32	3530	4.69	124018

Part II

	SSI Advances		NFS		OPS		Weaker		SC/ST	
	000	Rs	000	Rs	000	Rs	000	Rs	000	Rs
Bantwal	0.52	254985	1.21	39991	4.65	36676	8.99	15102	1.51	12787
Belthangady	0.18	120824	0.6	55150	2.53	63450	7.26	15102	0.8	10003
Mangalore	4.49	3E+07	1.12	78672	13.92	111462	4.87	17583	0.68	15700
Puttur	0.31	169170	0.36	65367	2.34	72381	5.19	27846	0.6	98679
Sullia	0.12	5190	0.15	54200	2.41	29922	4.75	20155	0.52	18940
D.K.	5.61	296578	3.43	58508	25.84	82183	31.06	18393	4.1	13081

Table 5.8: IRDP, etc Advances in DK

Part I

IRDP ADVANCE (in Rs. ooo)		DRI ADVANCE (in Rs. ooo)		SF/FM ADVANCE (in Rs. ooo)		ARTISANS ADVANCE (in Rs. ooo)		OTHER WEAKER (in Rs. ooo)		WOMEN ADVANCE (in Rs. ooo)	
No	Rs.	No.	Rs.	No.	Rs.	No.	Rs.	No.	Rs.	000	Rs.
1.44	6878	185	5665	4.48	19544	0.87	11529	0.52	15663	2.44	19572
1.88	4460	32	2782	3.44	19610	0.42	36200	0.69	15200	1.4	34314
0.83	9752	231	3896	2.29	14054	0.27	656333	0.68	27894	7.49	50563
0.73	8921	414	24010	3.1	36125	0.14	22536	0.21	33774	1.28	33080
0.77	9879	23	2696	2.47	23229	0.15	5046	0.81	24749	0.84	35542
5.65	7170	885	13603	15.77	22599	1.86	25369	2.79	22042	13.45	40647

Part II

MASONRY		PMRY		OTHER GOVT.		% TO TOTAL		% OF PRIORITY	
000	Rs.	000	Rs.	000	Rs.	000	Rs.	000	Rs.
3.52	22457	0.44	33596	0.49	8988	3761	84.49	18.13	47.62
1.65	48562	0.26	49441	0.72	27000	28.57	65.47	18.77	62.71
7.35	96491	0.9	56824	0.53	22642	3.5	39.72	1	52.69
1.55	28018	0.18	72571	0.15	24603	45.12	73.47	16.75	54.79
0.58	41294	0.14	42158	0.12	30881	32.88	49.88	18.93	114.23
1.66	63878	0.92	50948	2	21462	11.59	47.09	5.08	54.24

Table 5.9: Activity-Wise demand and collection

Part I

	Crop culti	Minor Irrig	Land devt	Farm mech	Pl+Horti	AH/BD	AH/PF	Ah/other	Fish	For
Demand cr	278.8	53.1	50.5	28.7	109.4	19.2	54.5	14.5	162.8	5.4
Collection cr	236.7	40.7	36.6	23.8	96.5	13.9	14.8	6.7	72.4	3.4
% Recovery	84.92	76.6	72.49	83.09	88.21	72.31	27.23	46.01	44.45	62.13
Balance(cr)	42.05	12.4	13.08	4.09	12.9	5.3	39.7	7.8	90.5	2.1
% O.D	15.08	23.4	27.51	16.91	11.79	27.69	72.77	53.99	55.55	37.87
Demand	217.9	128.1	42.5	40.1	17.6	14.2	5.6	0.9	19.3	*
Collection	2097.9	96.8	32.3	32.8	12.1	11.7	3.9	0.8	12.7	*
% Recovery	98.59	75.55	75.95	81.73	69.06	82.22	69.52	91.01	65.99	*
Balance(cr)	30.1	31.3	10.2	7.3	5.4	2.5	1.7	0.1	6.6	*
% O.D	1.41	24.45	24.05	18.27	30.94	17.78	30.48	8.99	34.01	*
Demand	497.7	113.7	88.1	156.1	18.6	488.9	4.4	0.22	2.6	*
Collection	431.6	80.6	71.4	153.3	12.2	483.2	4.2	0.2	2	*
% Recovery	86.7	70.92	81.1	98.25	65.89	98.83	95.02	90.91	76.06	*
Balance(cr)	66.2	33.1	16.7	2.7	6.3	5.7	0.2	0.02	0.6	*
% O.D	13.3	29.08	18.99	1.75	34.11	1.17	4.98	9.09	23.94	*
Demand	28.6	108.5	83.4	43.8	12.4	14.9	17.4	0.2	*	*
Collection	2886.9	87.2	67.1	39.8	10.3	10.4	17.3	*	*	*

Contd........

Table 5.9 (Part-I) Contd.......

	Crop culti	*Minor Irrig*	*Land devt*	*Farm mech*	*Pl+Horti*	*AH/BD*	*AH/PF*	*Ah/other*	*Fish*	*For*
% Recovery	98.58	80.42	80.51	90.8	83.17	69.57	99.65	*	*	*
Balance(cr)	41.7	21.2	16.3	4	2.1	4.5	0.1	0.2	*	*
% O.D	1.42	19.58	19.49	9.2	16.83	30.43	0.35	100	*	*
Demand	1148.7	88.3	132.5	22.7	5.8	10.3	6.2	1.4	*	*
Collection	1081.6	56	93.7	19.1	2.9	6.2	2.2	0.6	*	*
% Recovery	94.16	63.35	70.67	84.38	61.13	60.18	34.62	43.75	*	*
Balance(cr)	67.1	32.4	38.9	3.5	2.8	4.1	4	0.8	*	*
% O.D	5.84	36.65	29.33	15.62	48.87	39.82	65.38	56.25	*	*
Demand	6981.7	491.6	397	291.3	163.8	547.5	88.1	17.3	184.1	5.4
Collection	6734.6	361.2	301.1	268.8	134.1	525.3	42.4	8.3	87.1	3.4
% Recovery	96.46	73.48	75.83	92.2	81.94	95.95	48.12	48.2	47.14	62.13
Balance(cr)	247.1	130.4	96	22.5	29.6	22.2	45.7	8.9	97.6	2.1
% O.D	3.54	26.52	24.17	7.72	18.06	4.05	51.58	51.8	52.86	37.87

Table 5.9.1: Activity-Wise demand and collection

Part II

	Smy	*ALD*	*NFS*	*SSI*	*OPS*	*NPS*	*IRDP*	*PMRY*	*Other Pr*	*Total(Cr)*
Demand cr	1.1	1103	216.2	9800	3515	34260	44.1	195.3	33	496.7
Collection cr	1.1	1075	159.4	8968	2574	29985	26.1	95.2	18.6	433.1
% Recovery	98.23	97.53	73.75	91.5	73.23	87.52	79.11	48.75	56.4	87.2
Balance(cr)	0.02	27.2	56.7	832.6	941	4275	18.1	100.1	14.4	12.81
% O.D	1.77	2.47	26.25	8.5	26.77	12.48	40.89	51.25	43.6	12.81
Demand	3.4	58.2	43.9	71.3	577.9	706.7	37.5	30.5	8.2	38.58
Collection	3	46	27.8	27	483.4	615.5	25.6	16.6	4.8	35.04
% Recovery	89.85	79.08	63.49	37.82	83.63	87.09	68.38	54.54	58.58	90.83
Balance(cr)	0.4	12.2	16.1	44.3	99.5	91.2	11.9	13.9	3.4	3.54
% O.D	10.15	20.92	36.71	62.18	16.35	121.9	31.62	45.46	41.42	9.17
Demand	1.8	85.3	122.2	54.6	462.7	377.2	41	31.6	5.7	2.74
Collection	1.5	69	106	48.4	404.7	330.3	27	23.8	5	21.99
% Recovery	81.97	80.97	86.71	88.74	87.46	87.56	65.86	75.24	87.54	88.86
Balance(cr)	0.3	16.2	16.2	6.1	58	46.9	14	7.8	0.7	2.76
% O.D	18.03	19.03	13.29	11.26	12.54	12.44	34.14	24.76	12.46	11.14
Demand	3.2	48.4	10.1	16.9	278.8	378.6	39.3	29.7	6.7	39.45
Collection	2.8	40.4	8.3	7	231.8	322.6	24.3	17.9	4.3	37.32

Contd........

Table 5.9 (Part-II) Contd.......

	Smy	*ALD*	*NFS*	*SSI*	*OPS*	*NPS*	*IRDP*	*PMRY*	*Other Pr*	*Total(Cr)*
% Recovery	87.94	83.47	81.83	41.64	83.14	85.22	61.7	60.19	64.82	94.6
Balance(cr)	0.4	8	1.8	9.9	47.9	56	15.1	11.8	2.4	2.1
% O.D	12.06	16.53	18.18	58.36	16.86	14.78	38.3	39.81	35.18	5.4
Demand	*	20.1	59.2	169.7	598.1	423	24.4	38.2	6.6	26.86
Collection	*	17.4	49.4	91.2	478.5	389.5	17	29.9	5	22.88
% Recovery	*	86.53	83.5	53.72	80	92.1	69.65	57.24	75.38	85.19
Balance(cr)	*	2.7	9.8	78.6	119.6	33.4	7.4	16.3	1.6	4
% O.D	*	13.47	16.5	46.28	20	7.9	30.35	42.76	24.62	4.81
Demand	9.5	1314	451.5	10113	5432	36146	186.3	325.3	60.2	626.4
Collection	8.4	1248	350.8	9141	4172	316.4	120	175.4	37.7	550.3
% Recovery	88.69	94.95	77.7	90.39	76.8	87.54	64.39	53.9	62.67	87.86
Balance(cr)	1.1	66.3	100.7	971.4	126.1	4502	66.4	150	22.5	76.04
% O.D	11.31	5.05	22.3	9.41	23.2	1246	35.61	46.1	37.33	12.14

Table 5.10: Bankwise Demand and Collection

Bantwal

	Per branch (lakh)		Crop%		MI%		NFs%		SSI%		OPS%		NSS%		IRDP%		PMRY%	
Banks	DD	Rec	DD	Rec	DD	Rec	DD	Rec	DD	Rec	DD	Rec	DD	Rec	DD	Rec	DD	Rec
SBI	174.7	85.8	34.3	94	3.6	84.6	0	0	9.4	79.6	27.4	78.9	0	0	0.2	60	2.1	64.6
Canara Syndicate	88.3	73.8	20.9	84.4	8.7	62.3	2.1	70.4	3.7	70.3	22.2	68.6	20.9	90.7	2.3	42.6	2.6	49.4
Corporation	75.3	88.7	4.8	100	0.8	65.5	0.4	63.7	0	0	76.7	94.2	8.2	86	1.1	59.3	3.2	46.7
Vijaya	132.2	62.2	26	59.5	11.9	48.2	1.2	42.8	1.4	53.3	23.3	68.2	27.2	70	2.2	51.7	2.4	61.5
NGB	68.5	77	39.5	77	12.2	73.7	0.3	28	3.5	67	32.6	76.3	4.6	84	2.6	78	—	—
Karnataka	32.6	35.7	8.6	11.1	2.4	78.2	0	0	19.6	53.4	46.7	47.1	5.1	7.2	5	100	17.6	80.5
SCDCC	330.4	91	74.4	100	11	100	0.6	79.8	0	0	9.4	47.5	14.1	85.8	0.8	100	—	—
Total	3626.4	76	43.9	86.7	7.1	52.2	1.2	70.2	1.9	65.3	18.9	67.6	15.7	77.6	1.2	285.2	1.3	51.8

Contd.......

Table 5.10 Contd........

Mangalore

Banks	Per branch (lakh)		Crop%		MI%		NFs%		SSI%		OPS%		NSS%		IRDP%		PMRY%	
	DD	Rec	DD	Rec	DD	Re	DD	Rec	DD	Rec	DD	Rec	DD	Rec	DD	Rec	DD	Rec
SBI	48.9	65.8	4.8	98	0	0	0	0	13.8	58.6	52.9	71.5	26.7	61.4	0.02	67	0.3	43
SBM	47.3	80.5	0.1	78	0.6	25	1.6	84	9.6	70	53.3	90	23	83.3	0.04	75	3.3	73
Syndicate	426.1	66.2	0.1	51.5	0.1	60.8	0.9	71.4	13.2	68.4	10.2	70.4	73.1	81	0.1	57.7	0.5	46.3
Corporation	115	73.1	0.8	79	0.4	74.5	1.1	60.5	10.3	55.4	51	66.5	3.8	88.4	0.1	73	1.8	50
Vijaya	67.8	65.9	6.8	55.1	0.8	44.9	0.7	63.2	4.4	46.2	46.1	63.8	29.3	70.1	1.7	25.8	3.4	47.7
Canara	475.3	66.2	1.3	70.9	0.02	24	0.1	71.3	59.5	48.3	22.2	69.5	12.6	71.2	0.1	85	0.4	51.1
Others	366.1	59.9	3	75.7	0.6	82	6.7	54.3	8.3	43.8	34.6	67.3	41.7	60.5	0.1	80..7	0.6	38.6
Total	32166	72.7	1.5	90.2	0.2	66.4	1.9	73.9	26.7	62.5	23.7	75.4	42.3	79.4	0.2	45.6	0.7	42.7

Contd........

Table 5.10 Contd........

Puttur

	Per branch (lakh)		Crop%		MI%		NFs%		SSI%		OPS%		NSS%		IRDP%		PMRY%	
Banks	*DD*	*Rec*	*DD*	*Rec*	*DD*	*Re*	*DD*	*Rec*	*DD*	*Rec*	*DD*	*Rec*	*DD*	*Rec*	*DD*	*Rec*	*DD*	*Rec*
SBI																		
Canara	353.4	73	17.2	68.2	0	0	0	0	40.2	47	33.9	76.5	0	0	0	0	0	0
Syndicate	165.1	76.2	11.1	64.7	6.2	73.6	0.9	91.5	7.2	54	23.5	72.8	29.1	86	1.6	50.8	1.6	70.8
Corporation	11	80.2	47.3	94.8	3.4	46	18.9	51.9	0	0	8.9	83.7	0	0	0	0	0	0
Vijaya	75.6	62.6	39.8	69.5	16.2	49.4	1.4	75.5	1.6	52	21.3	68.4	6.8	76	2.7	68.8	1.3	46.3
NGB	112.7	83.5	29.3	76.5	15.7	78.5	0.1	27	3	83.5	23.6	92.5	12.8	91	0.7	44	0	0
Karnataka	84.2	101	2.8	88.7	1.2	101	0	0	0	0	42.9	98.9	34.4	106.4	0	0	0	0
SCDCC	790.2	95	85.4	100	0.6	100	0.1	85.3	0	0	7.1	87.3	4.1	81.7	0.03	100	0	0
PCARD	418.9	52.6	0	0	33.6	63.1	3.1	42.5	0	0	43.9	44.4	0	0	0	0	0	0
SBM	65.1	80.1	1.2	55.8	7.2	62.7	22.4	73	6.1	82.3	39	84.2	16.2	90.1	0.2	63.6	0.6	61.5
Total	6981.6	87.7	55.7	96.4	4.9	69.6	0.7	71	5.4	60.9	16.7	76	7.9	91.4	0.5	77.1	0.3	62

Contd........

Table 5.10 Contd........

Sullia

Banks	Per branch (lakh)		Crop%		MI%		NFs%		SSI%		OPS%		NSS%		IRDP%		PMRY%	
	DD	Rec	DD	Rec	DD	Re	DD	Rec	DD	Rec	DD	Rec	DD	Rec	DD	Rec	DD	Rec
Canara	205.6	82.7	18.2	95.3	2.3	76.3	0.1	69.8	0.7	83.7	19.2	18.7	43.8	85	0.4	56.5	1.2	73.6
Syndicate	92.9	58	24.6	68.4	11.2	51.2	0.4	34.3	1.4	45	16.8	62.5	7.7	68.3	2.8	44.3	1.8	36.7
Corporation	245.6	87.1	19.5	86.5	4.6	78.7	2.9	75.4	0.9	75.9	21.7	80.7	37.9	95.1	0.3	20.3	1	51.1
Vijaya	100.5	73.5	35.5	80	15.2	63.2	0.1	66.5	1	67.7	19.2	61.8	9.4	65.8	2.1	69	2.9	58.3
NGB	55.4	88	37.5	74.6	5.5	68	0.6	100	2.9	93.7	17.4	91	9.8	93	0	0	0	0
SCDCC	1103	98.7	88.8	100	0.6	100	0.1	40	0.1	100	3.2	89	6.2	86.5	0.2	100	0	0
PCARD	143.7	66.5	0	0	22.3	67.5	4.3	63.7	0	0	40.1	68.9	0	0	0.2	100	0	0
Others	59.2	90.8	3	57.4	4.8	50.6	0	0	67.8	100	21.3	81.7	0	0	0	0	4	48.7
Total	50993	76.5	19.7	94.3	2.14	63	1.6	73.6	18.2	61.8	21.2	74.7	30.9	79.8	0.43	98.7	0.83	46.4
All	5645.5	88.4	61.8	97.6	4.2	67	0.8	64.9	1.1	86	10.2	76.6	12	78.8	0.7	56.9	0.7	52.3

Table 5.11 : Service area Recovery and Outstanding (Half yearly) in percentage (September 1999)

		Bantwal	Belthangady	Mangalore	Puttur	Sullia	D.K.
Agriculture	% A/c	39.0	43.1	22.0	10.01	65.8	29.8
	% Amount	24.7	40.0	14.7	5.1	60.4	17.0
NFs and SSI	% A/c	4.2	4.0	2.8	8.6	5.1	5.2
	% Amount	15.3	3.9	10.2	20.5	10.1	5.2
OPS	% A/c	28.9	24.4	23.9	27.6	18.0	25.4
	Amount	31.5	32.8	17.7	25.1	14.0	23.6
NPS	% A/c	27.9	28.5	51.3	53.8	11.1	39.6
	Amount	28.5	23.3	57.4	49.3	15.0	44.7

Banks		*SBI*	*Canara*	*Corp*	*Syndi*	*Vijaya*	*Karn*	*Netrav*	*ARD+*
Total Advance	A/c	2.0	12.6	10.0	17.7	23.2	6.7	3.5	15.2
	Amount	2.3	17.1	13.3	13.4	12.9	11.9	1.4	15.3
Agriculture	% A/c	15.4	19.0	9.1	29.9	43.8	4.8	57.9	39.31
	Amount	12.2	11.67	5.4	15.7	27.7	4.3	41.7	39.9
NFS & SSI	% A/c	7.6	5.7	3.0	2.5	2.7	3.9	8.2	31.43
	Amount	11.1	16.3	8.0	16.7	5.6	14.7	10.9	34.81
Other priority Sector	% A/c	33.0	35.0	28.4	24.8	23.7	22.1	12.5	16.0
	Amount	29.8	25.7	22.2	20.0	24.7	15.6	24.9	21.7
NPS	% A/c	44.0	40.3	59.5	42.8	29.8	69.2	21.4	0.9
	Amount	46.9	46.3	64.4	47.6	42.0	65.4	22.5	11.7

Table 5.12 : Demand and recovery of loans in taluks

	Bantwal	*Belthan*	*Mangalore*	*Puttur*	*Sullia*	*D.K.*
Demand (%)	4.3	4.0	79.3	6.2	6.2	62.64 (Rs. bil)
% recovery	85.2	88.9	87.2	90.8	94.6	87.8
% O.D.	14.8	11.1	12.8	9.2	5.4	12.2
CL dd %	16.45	7.13	4.0	30.48	41.94	11.14
% sec	42.77	20.13	5.61	55.16	74.24	
% OD	94.16	86.70	84.92	98.59	98.58	96.46
MI	18.0	23.1	10.8	26.0	22.1	0.77
LD	33.4	22.2	12.7	10.7	21.0	0.63
FM	7.8	53.6	9.8	13.8	15.0	0.46
Pl-Hor	3.5	11.4	66.8	10.7	7.6	0.26
AH	2.7	75.6	13.5	3.2	5.0	1.03
Fish	-	1.5	88.1	10.4	-	0.29
ALD	1.6	6.5	83.8	4.4	3.7	2.09
NFS	13.1	27.1	47.9	9.7	2.2	0.72
SSI	1.7	0.5	96.9	0.7	0.2	16.13
OPS	11.0	8.5	64.8	10.6	5.1	8.66
NPS	1.2	1.0	94.8	2.0	1.0	56.91

Source: Syndicate Bank Lead Bank data

Table 5.13 : Service Area Recovery and Outstanding in percentage (September 1999)

Item		*D.K*	*Puttur*	*Mangalore*	*Beltha-ngady*	*Bantwal*	*Sullia*
Total Priority Sector Advance	A/c	59.8	39.0	50.3	73.3	72.7	82.1
	Amount	54.3	40.9	55.0	75.6	70.6	82.7
Total Advance for Agriculture	A/c	30.9	8.2	18.7	46.7	39.6	47.7
	Amount	17.0	5.9	13.1	40.6	26.0	52.4
Total Advance to SSI and NFS	A/c	7.7	12.1	4.9	8.7	8.2	7.2
	Amount	17.9	23.5	13.7	9.1	18.5	13.8
Total Advance to OPS	A/c	21.2	18.7	26.7	17.9	24.9	27.2
	Amount	19.4	11.5	28.2	25.9	26.1	16.5
Total Advance Under IRDP	A/c	8.0	3.1	2.9	15.2	16.4	11.3
	Amount	1.0	0.2	0.3	3.8	3.3	1.9
Total Advance Under PMRY	A/c	1.6	1.4	1.5	1.4	2.1	1.3
	Amount	1.2	0.8	0.9	2.3	3.1	1.3
Others	A/c	30.6	56.5	45.3	10.1	8.8	5.3
	Amount	43.5	58.1	43.8	18.3	23.0	14.1

Source: Syndicate Bank lead Bank data

Table 5.14 : Outstanding advances blockwise for IRDP and other programmes-2000-01

	IRDP		*PMRY*		*Other Govt Prog*		*Total*	
	No	*Amount*	*No*	*Amount*	*No*	*Amount*	*No*	*Amount*
Bantwal								
Total Branch	1438	9891	438	14715	493	4431	2369	29037
Per branch	59.92	412.13	18.25	613.13	20.54	184.63	98.71	1209.88
Belthangady								
Total Branch	1881	8389	263	13003	715	1905	2859	40697
Per branch	117.56	524.31	16.44	812.69	44.69	1206.56	178.69	2543.56
Mangalore								
Total branch	829	8084	899	51085	525	11887	2253	71056
Per branch	9.53	92.92	10.33	587.18	6.03	136.63	25.90	816.74
Puttur								
Total Branch	730	6512	182	13208	146	3592	1058	23312
Per branch	42.94	383.06	10.71	776.94	9.59	211.29	62.24	1371.29
Sullia								
Total branch	774	7646	139	5860	118	3644	1031	17150
Per branch	59.54	588.15	10.69	450.77	9.08	280.31	79.31	1319.23
D.K								
Total branch	5652	40522	1921	97871	1997	42859	9570	181252
Per branch	235.5	1688.42	80.04	4077.96	83.21	1785.79	398.75	7552.17

Source: Syndicate Bank, Mangalore Lead Bank data

Table 5.15 : Percent Share in Advances -talukwise: 2000-01

	Total Advances	Bantwal	Belthangady	Mangalore	Puttur	Sullia	D.K.
	No	17195	10741	68275	16925	9743	122879
	Rs. '000	748786	583752	8533100	862550	505506	11233694
Priority	No	81.16	70.35	33.95	68.00	81.64	52.25
Sector	Rs.	84.50	65.47	39.72	73.47	49.89	47.10
Agriculture	No	44.09	39.55	5.34	66.94	54.22	26.15
	Rs.	37.61	28.58	3.50	45.12	32.88	11.60
Direct	No	42.65	35.04	5.30	66.54	26.12	23.25
Agriculture	Rs.	25.61	25.37	1.96	15.42	16.09	6.42
Indirect	No	1.44	4.51	0.05	1.46	28.10	3.03
Agriculture	Rs.	12.00	3.21	1.54	29.71	16.79	5.18
SSI	No	3.02	1.69	6.57	1.81	1.18	4.56
	Rs.	17.67	3.77	17.00	6.00	1.18	14.81
Nfs	No	7.02	5.59	1.64	2.14	1.49	2.79
	Rs.	6.45	5.67	1.03	2.74	1.55	1.79
OPS	No	27.03	23.52	20.40	13.80	24.75	21.03
	Rs.	22.76	27.46	18.19	19.60	14.27	18.91
Weaker	No	52.29	67.57	7.14	30.66	48.73	25.28
	Rs.	18.13	18.78	1.00	16.7	18.93	5.09
SC/ST	No	8.79	7.40	0.99	3.53	5.31	3.34

Source: Syndicate Bank, Lead Bank data

Table 5.16: Service Area Recovery and Outstanding statement. June 1999 (in % age)

Item		*D.K*	*Puttur*	*Manga lore*	*Beltha-ngady*	*Bant wal*	*Sullia*
Total Priority Sector Advance	A/c	59.8	41.8	43.0	73.1	77.2	71.4
	Amount	55.9	44.9	49.3	76.6	75.5	76.4
Total Advance for Agriculture	A/c	31.4	11.4	11.9	45.9	53.8	39.7
	Amount	17.7	7.8	8.9	36.4	37.8	46.8
Total Advance to SSI and NFS	A/c	6.8	29.2	6.1	8.2	4.2	13.9
	Amount	19.9	20.5	22.5	9.9	15.5	12.7
Total Advance to Other Priority	A/c	21.6	21.2	25.9	19.0	19.2	17.8
	Amount	18.3	16.6	17.9	30.3	22.2	16.9
Total Advance Under IRDP	A/c	8.0	4.6	3.0	16.5	13.3	13.8
	Amount	1.2	0.4	0.2	6.3	3.	1.9
Total Advance Under PMRY	A/c	1.4	1.7	1.4	1.4	1.6	1.9
	Amount	1.2	1.3	0.8	2.8	2.7	1.3
Others	A/c	30.8	51.9	52.6	9.0	7.9	12.9
	Amount	41.7	53.4	49.7	14.3	18.3	20.4

Source: SyndicateBank, Lead Bank data

Table 5.17: Bankwise service area recovery and outstanding in DK (June 1999)

		Items	*SBI*	*Canara*	*Corp*	*Syndi*	*Vijaya*	*Karn.*	*Netra*
Total Advance	R	3.1	10.8	8.1	19.7	19.4	6.2	2.8	14.4
	O	5.4	17.9	10.6	22.4	8.5	8.8	1.0	12.1
Total Priority	R	50.4	61.5	35.3	52.1	70.8	28.1	89.0	74.2
Sector Advance	O	58.8	58.4	33.6	46.5	64.8	41.1	77.0	92.5
Total Advance	R	16.5	19.2	7.5	24.6	45.2	4.1	60.2	46.6
Agriculture	O	10.7	7.6	5.7	11.5	30.9	5.0	43.1	55.3
Total Advance	R	16.5	13.9	3.7	9.0	2.4	4.1	17.6	3.0
to SSI Sector	O	35.3	37.7	9.6	24.3	4.6	19.4	26.9	4.4
Total Advance to	R	17.3	28.4	24.1	18.5	23.2	19.9	3.1	24.6
O.P.S	O	12.8	13.1	18.3	10.7	29.3	16.7	7.0	32.8
Total Advance	R	4.2	5.3	4.2	10.6	15.8	1.0	20.5	0.6
Under IRDP	O	0.3	0.3	0.3	0.9	5.2	0.1	11.9	0.4
Total Advance	R	2.8	2.1	1.7	1.4	2.1	1.4	0	0
Under PMRY	O	1.3	0.9	1.2	1.0	4.3	0.8	0	0
Others Including NPS	R	39.6	40.4	64.9	51.6	25.7	58.0	11.1	7.1

Table 5.18: Service area Outlay to priority sector in DK (2002-03)-Rs in crore

Sector	*Service Area*	*Non-service Area*	*Total*	*% of Total Outlay*
Agrl + Allied	126.7	30.0	156.7	19.0
Crop loan	87.7	9.7	97.4	—
Rural Artisans + SSI	11.9	176.3	188.2	22.0
Trade + Service	54.3	166.1	220.4	26.0
Priority Sector	193.0	372.3	565.3	67.0
Non-prio Sector	52.8	225.5	278.3	33.0
All Sectors	245.8	597.8	843.6	100.0

Source: Syndicate Bank, District credit Plan for D K district 2002-03

Lead District Office, Mangalore

6
CONCLUSION

Suit Filed Cases

In Dakshina Kannada during 2000-01, a total number of 1572 cases were pending for recovery, the amount being Rs. 15.4 crore according to the data provided by the lead district manager. Of this, over 90 per cent was pending at the start of the year and the rest filed during the year. The share of different banks in this has been: Syndicate bank 49 per cent , Canara bank 17 per cent , Karnataka bank 13 per cent , Vijaya bank 6.5 per cent , Corporation, SBI and SCDCC bank each over 3 per cent the other banks accounting for about 5 per cent. During the year, about 20 per cent of the cases have been disposed of, the amount being 15.6 per cent. Of the total disposed amount, the share of Syndicate bank has been over 65 per cent. During 2001-02, the number of pending cases under PDRR has been Rs. 54.8 crore of less than one year (for 380 cases) and Rs. 32.45 crore under more than one year (for 338 cases), bringing the total to over Rs. 87.5 crore. Of this, the share of SCDCC bank has been more than 90 per cent. The number of cases pending other than PDDR of less than one year have been 367 with an amount of Rs. 18.3 crore (Vijaya bank having the bulk) and of over one year 214 cases with an amount of Rs. 6.9 crore, bringing the total to Rs. over Rs. 25 crore (Syndicate and Canara banks having the bulk share). The amount of total pending cases-Rs 112.5 crore is 10 per cent of total advances which is a serious matter to be looked into by the banking sector. It may be seen that with the onslaught of internet banking, these cases may subside over the years.

The Internet Era

In this emerging internet era, apart from the speed and quality of information provided by e-banking and other internet banking instruments, one of the major developments has been reduction in cost, which is yet to be fully realized in Indian conditions. According to Furst et al (2002), internet-banks have outperformed non-internet banks in terms of profitability, more aggressive business. However *de novo* internet banks under-performed in these respects when compared to non-internet *de novos.* Of course, banks with a longer history of internet banking fare well owing to absence of start-up costs in new investment, and training, and these have the capacity to offer a wide range of products when compared to small start-up banks. Since the percentage of customers using internet banking is very small and also owing to the fact that the internet banks offer a limited number of products in the country, internet revolution in the banking sector will take some time to fructify. The transformation of traditional banks into modern ones will take its own adoption period. In the more developed countries where the internet change has started since 1995, it took three to four years for many banks to be completely internetted and in India, the pace may take at least double the time.

Conclusion

For the Indian banking industry to be strong and globally competitive, emphasis on market discipline and adoption of international standards become crucial. Further, management of organizational change and consolidation within the financial system along with upgradation of technological infrastructure and human resource development. According to Jalan (2002a), by the end of March 2002, 25 out of 27 PSBs have had risk weighted capital adequacy ratios above the norm of 9 per cent , while in 23 the ratio was in excess of 10 per cent. The banks have undertaken offering equities and issuance of subordinated debt for inclusion under capital tier II. As the 90-day norm in loan impairment is to take effect from 2005 in all financial systems, provisioning and changed interest rates on monthly rests have been resorted to. Exposure norms are linked to capital with refinement of asset-liability management system. The Stern-Stewart Co "economic value added" framework will make best use of capital by calculation of net operating profit less adjusted taxes, invested capital and weighted average cost of capital.

In the case of non-performing assets, much has to be done to bring the level to the international standard norm of 2 per cent. It is opined that 43 per cent of cumulative provisioning for losses is low when compared to international standards (Jalan 2002a). The recently passed Securitization and Reconstruction of Security Interest Act enables for the enforcement of security interest, dispute settlement and penalties in order to improve the financial system of the banks. The establishment of Credit Information Bureau enables economizing on production costs associated with supply of information regarding financial matters and to close the gap between economic and accounting valuations. The investment fluctuation reserve will enable the banks to maximize their gains from investments, which are on the rise.

In spite of the above, Sharma (2001) highlights the fact that Indian banks are subject to low degree of regulation when compared to those in developed countries and that especially in the exit (of ailing banks) policy and quotes Barth et al (1998) who analyzed the following activities of the banks in this respect:

1. underwriting of securities, brokering, dealing and mutual fund business
2. underwriting of insurance and selling
3. real estate investment and management and
4. non-financial firm ownership and control

Their major conclusion is that weaker the governance, harsher would be the restrictions on the banks to indulge in the above activities without restraints. However, no relationship has been found between restriction and financial development. They find that restriction of security-related activities of banks increases bank crises. As regards regulation of entry, market discipline, disclosures, compulsory audit, capital requirements, exit provisions and range of allowable activities is concerned, Sharma (2001) points out that regulation severity is seen in respect of capital requirements and allowable activities in India when compared to other countries, whereas in respect of disclosure, audit and exit provisions, much has to be accomplished.

Whatever be the intensity of NPAs, especially when viewed from the failure of some large corporations which have got funding from the banks, banking sector stocks have a faster growth of earnings share and mergers and acquisitions valuations. The recent government buyback of illiquid high interest securities and the raising of FDI limit to 74 per cent from the existing 49 per cent level will facilitate larger funds flow in banks and buyback opportunity to local shareholders. Further, capital appreciation in government securities, also due to decline in interest rates has improved the profit ratio of the banks. The proposal to reduce government stake in PSBs to 33 per cent and the entry of FIIs will boost up the prospects of the banks especially in retail banking. Hence, it can be said that the Indian banks, especially PSBs seem to have a bright future, while some of the foreign banks are closing their shop due to various reasons. In a way, increasing budget and trade deficits in poor countries have resulted in government divestment and privatization of banking and other sectors rather than for the sake of privatization as such.

Nowadays, a lot of importance is placed on good corporate governance, especially after the International Accounting Standards, US Generally accepted Accounting Principles (not as successful as IAS) and the US Sarbanes-Oxley Act, wherein senior officers of a company have been credited with the responsibility of creation of good corporate culture. In India, the Audit Committee of the Board oversees risk management practices. According to National Association of Corporate Directors, self-evaluation by the board has been suggested. Finally, retail banking with total relationship value in different fields can make the banks realize their new social commitment.

REFERENCES

Barth J, Caprio G and Levine R 2001. "The Regulation and Supervision of Banks around the World: A New Database", PRWP 2588, Development Economics Department, World Bank, Washington D C.

Barth J R, Caprio Jr G and Levine R 1998. "Financial Regulation and Performance: Cross Country Evidence", World Bank Policy Research Working Paper 2037, Washington.

Besley T 1997. 'Political Economy of Alleviating Poverty: Theory and Institutions', *Annual World Bank Conference on Development Economics*, The World Bank, Washington D C, pp 117-34.

Business India, 2002. Best Banks, Business India, Nov 25 to Dec 8, 2002.

Caprio Jr, G and D Klingebiel, 1997. "Bank Insolvency: Bad Luck, Bad policy or Band Banking?', *Annual World Bank Conference on Development Economics*, World Bank, Washington DC, pp. 79-104.

Centre for Monitoring Indian Economy, 2000. Banking Statistics, CMIE, Mumbai.

Clare G, Cull R, Peria M S M and Sanchez S M 2003. "Foreign Bank Entry: Experience, Implications for Developing Economies, and Agenda for further Research" *The World Bank Research Observer*, 18:1, pp. 25-59.

Das M R, 2002. "An Objective Method for Ranking Nationalized Banks', *Prajnan*,31:2, pp. 111-36.

Dasgupta R 2002. "Priority Sector lending: Yesterday, Today and Tomorrow, *Economic and Political Weekly,* 37:41, pp. 4239-45.

Demirguc-Kunt, A and R Levine, 1996. "Stock markets, Corporate Finance and Economic Growth: an Overview, *The World Bank Economic Review,* 10:2, pp. 223-39.

Demirguc-Kunt, A and H Huizinga, 1999. "Determinants of Commercial Bank Interest Margins and Profitability: Some International Evidence, *The World Bank Economic Review,* 13:2, pp. 379-408.

Demirguc-Kunt A and Detragiache E, 2000." Monitoring Banking Sector Fragility: A Multivariate Logit Analysis", *The World Bank Economic Review,* 14:2, pp. 287-30.

Economic and Political Weekly, 2002. Money, Banking and Finance Special, 37:5.

Foss N and M Volker 2000. *Competence, Governance and Entrepreneurship: Advances in Economic Strategy Research,* Oxford University Press, New York.

Furst K, Lang W W and Nolle D E, 2002. " Internet Banking", *Journal of Financial Services Research,* 22:1/2, pp. 95-117.

Honohan, P 2002. "Comment on Costs of banking system instability: some empirical evidence", *Journal of Banking and Finance,* 26, pp. 857-60.

Jalan, B 2002. "Indian Banking and Finance: Managing New Challenges", *RBI Bulletin,* February, pp. 71-87.

Jalan, B 2002a. "Strengthening Indian Banking and Finance: Progress and prospects", Inaugural Address to 24th Bank Economists' Conference, Bangalore, December 27.

Jeanneau, S and M Micu 2002. "International Bank lending to Emerging Market countries", *BIS Quarterly Review,* March, pp. 52-64.

Jog C S, 2002. 'The Changing Scenario of Indian Banking-Vision 2025", *PNB Monthly Review,* 24:5, pp. 4-11.

Kamesan V, 2202. "Challenges before the Indian Banking Industry", *PNB Monthly Review,* 24:10, pp. 4-9.

Korzeniewicz R P and T P Moran 1997. 'World Economic Trends in the Distribution of Income 1965-90', *American Journal of Sociology*, 102, p 40.

Krugman P 1994. 'The Myth of Asia's Miracle' *Foreign Affairs*, Nov-Dec, pp 62-78.

Laeven L 2002. "Bank Risk and Deposit Insurance', *The World Bank Economic Review*, 16:1, pp. 109-37.

Mishkin, F S, 1997. "Banking Failures: Crisis or Opportunity for Reform?", *Annual World Bank Conference on Development Economics, 1996*, World Bank, Washington DC, pp.29-61.

Nachane, D M et al. "Bank response to Capital requirements", *Economic and Political Weekly*, 36:4, pp. 329-36.

Nambirajan, R 2000. "Performance of PSBs after reforms with reference to NPAs, *PNB Monthly Review*,22:10, pp. 5-14.

Reserve Bank of India, 2002. Banking Statistics, Supplement to December issue.

Sharma, A K, 2000. "Study of Major Banking aggregates of Scheduled Commercial Banks", *PNB Monthly Review*, 22:5, pp. 36-42 and 22:6, pp. 33-41.

Sharma, M 2001. "Benchmarking the Degree of regulation on Indian Banks: A Cross Country Study", *Prajnan*, XXX:2, pp. 185-98.

Sherman M and M Wanders 2002. "Build-to-order Banking in Asia", McKinsey and Company.

Swarnkar, C P 2002. "Contemporary Global trends in Banking", *PNB Monthly Review*, 24:1, pp.4-10.

Williamson O E 2000. "Strategy Research: Governance and Competence Perspectives", in Foss and Mahnke ed. op.cit. pp. 21-54.

Wolfe M 1996. *Elusive Development*, Vistaar Publications, New Delhi.

Wooldridge P D 2002. "The International Banking Market", *BIS Quarterly Review*, March, pp.16-24.

INDEX